MURTY CLASSIC
LIBRARY OF IND



# TULSIDAS
# THE SEA OF SEPARATION

TULSIDAS

# THE SEA OF SEPARATION

## *A Translation from the Ramayana of Tulsidas*

Translated by

PHILIP LUTGENDORF

MURTY CLASSICAL LIBRARY OF INDIA
HARVARD UNIVERSITY PRESS
Cambridge, Massachusetts
London, England
2024

Printed in the United States of America
First printing

First published in Murty Classical Library of India,
Volume 24, Harvard University Press, 2020.

SERIES DESIGN BY M9DESIGN

*Library of Congress Cataloging-in-Publication Data*
Tulasidasa, 1532–1623.
The epic of Ram / Tulsidas ; translated by Philip Lutgendorf.
volume cm. — (Murty Classical Library of India ; 24)
In English.
Includes bibliographical references.
ISBN 978-0-674-29566-7 (pbk.)
I. Lutgendorf, Philip, translator.
II. Tulasidasa, 1532–1623. Ramacaritamanasa. English.
III. Tulasidasa, 1532–1623. Ramacaritamanasa. IV. Title.
PK1947.9.T83R313 2016
891.4'312—dc23 2015016322

# CONTENTS

# INTRODUCTION

## *The* Rāmcaritmānas *and Tulsidas*

The *Rāmcaritmānas* by Tulsidas is among the most beloved and revered works of Indian literature.[1] An epic poem composed in Hindi in the late sixteenth century, the *Mānas* rapidly acquired the renown and sanctity usually reserved for compositions in Sanskrit, the ancient and elite "language of the gods." Over the next three centuries its fame grew steadily, spread by oral expounders, itinerant singers, and scholarly exegetes, some of whom were patronized by the princely rulers of the Indo-Gangetic Plain. In the colonial era, British scholars and administrators recognized it as "the Bible of Northern India" and "the best and most trustworthy guide to the popular living faith of its people."[2] In the twentieth century it assumed an important place in the emerging Hindi literary canon, inspired major works by modernist poets, and was regularly quoted during India's freedom struggle by Mohandas Gandhi, who wrote that he considered it "the greatest book of all devotional literature."[3] Later its impact was enhanced by the release of millions of inexpensive printed copies, by performances available on records, audiocassettes, and compact discs, and by a television serialization partially based on it that held much of India spellbound in 1987–1989. A comprehensive early twenty-first-century study of the development of Hindi literature assesses the *Mānas* as "a defining work of Indian culture" and concludes that it "remains the leading vernacular scripture of north India today."[4]

A retelling of the ancient and popular tale of Ram and Sita, which first appeared in literary form in Valmiki's Sanskrit epic *Rāmāyaṇa* (last centuries B.C.E.), the *Mānas* belongs to a long tradition of works that recast the narrative in distinctive ways. Despite the prestige accorded the Sanskrit archetype, subsequent retellings never favored literal translation. Instead, poets and storytellers working in Sanskrit, various Prakrits, and later regional literary vernaculars of southern and northern India exercised great freedom in crafting original versions that, while preserving the basic characters and outline of the narrative, introduced significant innovations. The result was a multiform oral and literary tradition that, although sometimes encompassed by the generic label "Ramayana," may better be termed *Rāmakathā*, or "Rama storytelling." Tulsidas's own version emerges from an influential current in this vast river of story, imbued with the ideology of "sharing" in or devotion to—*bhakti* is the Indic term—a personal god or goddess and the emotional, public worship of that deity.

A poet of extraordinary versatility and vision, Tulsidas is celebrated as the author of a dozen works, most of which are dedicated to Ram, and which collectively advance a theology in which Ram is adored as the supreme, transcendent God to whom other revered Hindu deities are ultimately subordinate. Through his writings and his legendary biography, Tulsidas has come to exert a profound and perhaps unsurpassed influence on the ideology and practice of popular Hinduism throughout much of northern and central India and beyond, including several communities of the Indian diaspora. Not surprisingly, a figure of such stature is also, in certain contexts, controversial; his works have been subject to vastly differing interpretations, and there are few details of his biography that have not been contested, beginning with his date of birth (variously posited as 1497, 1526, and 1543—the last being favored by the majority of modern scholars); a death date of 1623 is widely accepted. He was evidently literate—a few manuscripts survive that may be in his own hand—and seems to have received a classical Sanskrit education that was, in his day, generally the prerogative of the Brahman caste. Some of his works hint at autobiographical details, and three include dates of composition, indicating that he was active during the reigns of the Mughal emperors Akbar and Jahangir. There is evidence that he spent a good part of his life in Banaras, regularly participated in the public performance of devotional texts, including his own, and was supported in part by the offerings of appreciative listeners. His name means "servant of tulsi," referring to the "holy basil" plant considered especially pleasing to Vishnu, and thus signals the poet's likely initiation into a Vaishnava religious order or guru-lineage, *-dās* being a common suffix for initiatory names in several orders. The poet himself often shortens this name to "Tulsi" in his poetic "signature" (*chāp* or *bhaṇitā*). Yet although he has been proudly claimed by a number of branches of one ascetic order (the Ramanandis), Tulsi's formal affiliation has never been proven to the satisfaction of nonsectarian scholars. He does not seem to have established a sect, yet he came to be revered in his own lifetime as a *gosāĩ*, or "master"; today "Goswami" (in its standard Anglicized spelling) is typically prefixed to his name to indicate his status as preceptor and exemplar to millions.

Tulsi's most celebrated work, the *Rāmcaritmānas*, bears a date of composition corresponding to 1574. It comprises roughly 12,800 lines, divided into 1,073 "stanzas" set within seven sections, which early manuscripts simply denote as numbered "stairs" or "stairways" (*sopāna*)—"first stair," "second stair," and so on—descending into the allegorical Manas Lake to which the title alludes.[5] Later tradition has given them additional names as *kāṇḍs*, or sub-books, that reflect the architecture of the *Vālmīki Rāmāyaṇa*.

But apart from its basic storyline, the *Mānas* bears only an occasional direct resemblance to Valmiki's poem. Instead, drawing creatively on many sources, Tulsi retells the story of Ram, as he says, "for his own inner joy," through a set of four interlocking dialogues that ingeniously frame the epic tale.[6] The conversations between the gods Shiva and Parvati, the Vedic sages Yajnavalkya and Bharadvaj, the immortal crow Bhushundi and the divine eagle Garuda, and finally the discourse of Tulsidas to his presumed audience, interwoven throughout much of the text, are announced in the allegory of Lake Manas as its framing banks, or ghats. To traditional commentators, they suggest four distinct "points of view" from which the epic tale may be interpreted, even as they invoke a lineage of transmission that encourages future interpretive performances. A vibrant tradition of such performances—by storytellers and singers, and by amateur and professional actors who mount annual drama cycles collectively known as *Rāmlīlā* ("Ram's play")—has existed for centuries and remains influential in many parts of India today.

### *The Story Thus Far*

Tulsidas's narration of the epic tale of Ram begins roughly halfway through *Bālkāṇḍ*, the first and longest of his seven "stairways" or sub-books. It is preceded by an elaborate prologue in the poet's own voice, in which he seeks the blessings of gods, divine characters, and listeners, praises the spiritual power of Ram's name, and lays out the grand design of his epic with an allegory of sacred Lake Manas in the Himalayas. The Vedic sage Yajnavalkya then takes over as principal narrator, responding to a doubt voiced by another sage about whether the incarnate Ram, royal hero of a worldly saga, can truly be identical to the transcendent and supreme God. The affirmative answer includes a series of tales that set the stage for Ram's incarnation, as well as the long account of Lord Shiva's marriage to goddess Parvati, and the commencement of that god's own retelling of the Ram story in response to a similar doubt expressed by his consort.[7]

Responding to the tyranny of the demonic Ravan, the gods implore Lord Vishnu to take birth on earth, and accordingly Ram and his three brothers are born to Dasarath, king of Avadh, and his queens. After childhood adventures, Ram and his brother Lakshman enter the forest in the company of Sage Vishvamitra, slay demons who have been harassing the latter, and make their way to the adjacent kingdom of Videha where Ram, after meeting and falling in love with Princess Sita, wins her in marriage by lifting and breaking the divine bow of Shiva. *Bālkāṇḍ* ends with the spectacular and joyous nuptials of Ram and Sita.[8]

The second sub-book, *Ayodhyākāṇḍ*, begins with preparations for Ram's consecration as heir-apparent to the throne of Avadh. But these are soon thwarted by the machinations of a jealous junior queen, Kaikeyi, and her malicious maidservant. They demand that Dasarath, bound by an oath made long before, give the kingdom to Prince Bharat, Kaikeyi's son, and send Ram into forest exile for fourteen years. Ram obediently accepts this cruel sentence and leaves Avadh, accompanied, at their insistence, by Sita and Lakshman. Though it causes profound sorrow in the city, their departure and journey to the forest bring bliss to the villagers, sages, and tribal peoples they encounter on their way.

Separated from his favorite son, the king soon dies of grief, and Bharat, returning after a long absence, disavows his mother and refuses the throne. Instead, he retraces Ram's route to the forest of Chitrakut, followed by the entire court and citizenry, to beg Ram to return. When Ram, after protracted and emotional interactions, insists on fulfilling his father's promises and remaining in exile, Bharat and his entourage reluctantly return to Avadh bearing Ram's sandals. These the devoted junior prince, regarding himself as merely regent, places on the throne to await his beloved brother's promised return.[9]

### *"In the Forest," "The Kingdom of Kishkindha," and "The Beautiful Quest"*

Structurally, Tulsidas's epic presents a rough symmetry, with two lengthier *kāṇḍs* or sub-books (one and two, and six and seven) bracketing three shorter ones, and with the midmost (sub-book four) being the shortest of all. The three interior *kāṇḍs* are presented here in a single volume. Thematically, they encompass much of the drama of the years of Ram's exile: his violent and fateful encounters with demonic beings that will lead to the kidnapping of his wife, and his meeting and alliance with demidivine monkeys who will help him locate Sita and initiate the struggle to win her back. These key episodes, common to nearly all Ramayana retellings, are given characteristically distinctive interpretations by the poet, in keeping with his fervent devotion to Ram as the highest God.

Notably, these *kāṇḍs* also contain some of the epic's most controversial and debated episodes and passages. These include the mutilation of Ravan's sister Shurpanakha, Sita's abduction and Ram's ensuing grief, and the slaying by Ram of the monkey king Bali as a favor to Bali's younger brother, Sugriv, with whom Ram has formed an alliance. In addition, there are didactic passages—sometimes spoken by Ram himself—that rail against the temptations women present to men, champion deference to Brahmans irrespective of their character or merits, or criticize those relegated to the fourth social class of traditional society, the Shudras (serfs or peasants). In modern times, these verses have been much quoted by critics who accuse the *Mānas* author of misogyny and caste-based prejudice; in Tulsi's defense, his many admirers have offered various rationalizations for the troubling passages and have sometimes quoted other verses—including some from these same sub-books—that express apparently contradictory and egalitarian sentiments.[10] Indeed, these same *kāṇḍs* also include some of the most cherished and frequently read passages in the epic—particularly "The Beautiful Quest" (*Sundarkāṇḍ*) which today is recited by millions of people as an act of devotion to Ram's servant and devotee, Hanuman, who is himself worshiped as a major deity.[11]

The forty-six stanzas of "In the Forest" (*Araṇyakāṇḍ*) alternate thematically between two very different kinds of encounters with denizens of the wild lands that lay beyond the settled terrain of city and village. On the one hand, there are numerous meetings between Ram and reclusive ascetics—holy men and women who recognize his divinity and honor him with hymns of praise that sometimes introduce Sanskrit passages into the epic's standard Avadhi dialect. In counterpoint to these beatific interludes are narrative passages featuring violent encounters with demonic beings (*rākṣasas*), whose malevolence toward the holy ones Ram punishes, usually with death, and whose monarch, Ravan, eventually seeks revenge by stealing Ram's beloved wife.

At the beginning of this sub-book, Ram, Sita, and Lakshman leave Chitrakut, site of their emotional reunion with the royal family and citizens of Avadh, and move deeper into the forest. Their warm reception by four successive sages—Atri, Sharabhang, Sutikshan, and Agastya (and Anusuya, the wife of Atri, who lectures Sita on women's duties)—is followed by a metaphysical discourse by Ram to Lakshman, and then by their fateful encounter with Shurpanakha, Ravan's sister, who tries to seduce both Ram and his brother, threatens Sita's life, and has her nose and ears sliced off by Lakshman. This leads to Ram's first major battle with demonic hordes, and then to the scheme to kidnap Sita hatched by Ravan, reluctantly assisted by his uncle Marich, who becomes a magical deer to lure Ram and Lakshman away from Sita's side. The noble vulture Jatayu, mortally wounded trying to save Sita, is able to tell Ram something of her fate; he then dies and, honored with funerary rites by Ram, achieves a transfigured state. After slaying a monster named Kabandh (actually a demigod under a curse, who further guides the brothers in their quest), Ram meets the female tribal ascetic Shabari, to whom he discourses on the ninefold devotional path. Finally, he is visited by the divine sage Narad, to whom he preaches at length on the dangerous temptations of women, as well as on the greatness of saintly people.

As usual, some episodes told in great detail in other Ramayanas are presented by Tulsi in highly condensed form—thus the monstrous demon Viradh, whose assault and slaying occupy two chapters in Valmiki's forest book, is disposed of here in two lines.[12] Likewise Ram's anguish and near madness at his separation from Sita, vividly described in five chapters of the *Vālmīki Rāmāyaṇa*, is narrated by Tulsi in just five admittedly beautiful couplets.[13] Later, a two-stanza speech by the hero about the pain of his longing, set against the lushness of the monsoon season, is intermixed with apparent shame, anger, and warnings about the distractions, for men, of feminine allure.[14]

In these and other passages, Tulsi repeatedly reminds his audience that Ram, who is supreme God, is merely acting the part of a lovesick, suffering man for the sake of his salvific mission. The poet thus responds to the "doubt" expressed, in sub-book one, by the goddess Sati (and no doubt by others among Tulsi's contemporaries) concerning the divinity of a hero who could appear to be so human; indeed, Sati's misgivings were aroused precisely by glimpsing Ram's desperate search for his lost wife.[15] Tulsi's desire to exempt his divine characters from full participation in human experience and emotion may also explain one of this sub-book's most striking "innovations" in the story—though in fact it is also found in the earlier *Adhyātmarāmāyaṇa*.[16] This is Sita's substitution, at Ram's request, of a simulacrum of herself—a "shadow Sita"—while she conceals herself in the sacred fire of their hut. Though it occupies less than a stanza and is quickly forgotten, the so-called *māyā sītā* interlude technically spares Ram's divine consort the indignity of abduction and imprisonment, and will later allow for a different interpretation of the motive behind the "fire-test" of her chastity.[17]

At thirty stanzas, "The Kingdom of Kishkindha" (*Kiṣkindhākāṇḍ*) is the shortest of the epic's seven sections, and unlike the previous one, it introduces few digressions in its relatively straightforward narration of Ram's alliance with extraordinary monkeys and the initiation of their search for Sita. These monkeys have earlier been identified as gods who have taken birth in monkey form to assist in Ram's earthly task.[18] In their attributes and behavior they appear at times human or superhuman, and at others distinctly simian, preserving an ambiguity already present in the *Vālmīki Rāmāyaṇa*.[19]

As the *kāṇḍ* opens, the exiled and timid monkey prince Sugriv sends his minister Hanuman to Ram and Lakshman to determine whether they pose a threat. Hanuman brings the brothers to Sugriv and brokers an alliance based on a pledge of "mutual love."[20] Learning of Sugriv's cruel treatment by his elder brother, Bali, Ram stages a fight between the two and mortally wounds Bali; he then has Lakshman enthrone Sugriv and retreats to a camp on Mount Pravarshan for the duration of the rainy season. A long passage, spoken by Ram, describes the monsoon and his own suffering in his separation from Sita, and then the ensuing season of autumn. After a brief outburst of anger at Sugriv for apparently forgetting his promise to send out search parties, Ram oversees the dispatching of myriad monkeys to the four directions, giving special instructions and his signet ring to Hanuman and the southbound contingent. That party's adventures are then described, culminating in a dramatic meeting in a cavern with an aged ascetic woman who magically transports them to the shore of the southern ocean. Despairing of crossing it, the monkeys prepare to fast to death, until a vulture named Sampati restores their hope and tells them of Sita's whereabouts. The formidable challenge of a "hundred leagues" of ocean remains, but as the sub-book ends, the bear Jambavan reminds Hanuman, son of the wind, of his divine paternity and extraordinary powers, and the great monkey grows to immense size and prepares to leap across the sea.[21]

As always in Tulsidas, a mood of bhakti is pervasive; both Hanuman and Sugriv instantly recognize Ram's divinity, and the exiled monkey ruler only reluctantly agrees to resume his throne, for he would much prefer to renounce the world and worship at Ram's feet. And what was considered one of the Sanskrit Ramayana's most problematic passages—Bali's complaint against Ram for killing him from a place of concealment while Bali was engaged in combat with his brother—is similarly suffused with devotional sentiment.[22] Bali addresses Ram only briefly, "with love in his heart but harsh words on his lips," is quickly chastised, and then turns down Ram's own gracious offer to restore his life because he prefers the incomparable boon of dying in Ram's presence.[23]

Finally, "The Beautiful Quest" (*Sundarkāṇḍ*) presents in sixty stanzas the dramatic events that climax the search for Sita and initiate the effort to win her back. Like the comparable section of the *Vālmīki Rāmāyaṇa*, this sub-book has acquired special status among traditional audiences; it exists in numerous manuscripts and printed chapbook editions, excerpted from but independent of the larger epic, attesting to its evident popularity and ritualized recitation.[24] There has been much speculation over its title, for it is the only Ramayana section not named for a geographical locale, time period, or set of events, but there is no doubt that both the Sanskrit and Avadhi versions have been widely regarded as especially "beautiful," not only because of their fine poetry but also owing to their focus on some of the epic's most popular characters.[25]

In the course of leaping across the sea and entering Lanka,

Hanuman triumphs over three demonic obstacles. He then scours the city for Sita, encountering Ravan's junior brother Vibhishan, who is not only a virtuous *rākṣasa* but, here, already a fervent Ram devotee. Locating Sita in the royal Ashoka Grove, Hanuman witnesses her intimidation by Ravan and subsequent intention to immolate herself (there seems to be no hint that this desperate princess is the shadowy simulacrum created in sub-book three). Revealing himself, Hanuman delivers Ram's ring and message, along with much encouragement. Then, with Sita's permission, he feasts on the fruits of the garden, ransacking it in the process and killing legions of demon troops, including one of Ravan's sons. He is finally captured (with his own collusion) by Ravan's eldest, Meghnad, bound, and brought to the ten-headed king's court. There Hanuman berates and lectures Ravan, who then commands that his tail be set on fire. Escaping his bonds, Hanuman ingeniously uses his own punishment to further punish his captors by burning their golden city, before paying a final visit to Sita. Returning across the sea, he comforts first his search party compatriots and then Ram, who quickly sets out for the coast with Sugriv and a vast army of monkeys and bears. Meanwhile, in Lanka, Ravan scorns much good advice to return Sita to Ram and angrily expels Vibhishan, who crosses the sea and makes an emotional submission to the Raghu prince. Ram then petitions the sea god for safe passage to Lanka—an act of humility witnessed by Ravan's spies, who report to their master and again urge him to return the prince's wife. It takes Ram's wrath, however, to get a response from the sluggish marine deity, who reveals, at last, that two of the monkeys possess the skill to build a marvelous causeway of floating boulders that will enable the army to cross to Lanka.

Although "The Beautiful Quest" shares its poetic beauty with the rest of Tulsi's epic, it unquestionably contains many standout passages, and most of these occur within the first thirty-four stanzas, which are especially beloved by traditional audiences because they recount the "noble deeds of Hanuman" (*Hanumān carit*). Indeed, many of these passages are spoken by the "son of the wind" himself, who besides being immensely powerful is also extraordinarily eloquent. As in the Valmiki version, Hanuman delivers to Sita a heartfelt, stanza-long profession of Ram's love in an emotional tenor that far surpasses anything that Ram himself is elsewhere reported as having said.[26] He also gives a breathless, tour-de-force sermon to Ravan that constitutes a single prodigious sentence.[27] His ecstatic reunion with Ram includes a similarly charged love-message from Sita, likewise never spoken within the narrative by the princess that elicits tears from Ram, as well as the statement that "I can never repay my debt to you"—which, to Hanuman's many worshipers, stands as a divine promise guaranteeing his infallibility as an intercessor with Ram as transcendent God.[28]

There is another memorable promise made by Ram in this sub-book—one freighted with obvious theological import but also worth remembering in a Kali Yuga, or "age of discord," characterized by millions of displaced and traumatized people seeking political asylum and better lives: in accepting Vibhishan despite his own advisers' misgivings, Ram speaks of his vow "to allay the fears of refugees" and to offer "tender love" to all who seek his shelter, to which he adds this memorable couplet,

> Those who abandon seekers of refuge,
> calculating their own potential loss,
> are the vilest of people—sinners,
> the very sight of whom is harmful.[29]

The title of this volume is drawn from the poem and alludes to several important themes in these sub-books.[30] The fateful separation of Ram and Sita (though only illusory in Tulsi's retelling) occurs in the forest section and leads to much suffering for both hero and heroine, of which they and Hanuman speak eloquently in the following two sub-books.[30] The kidnapped Sita is, of course, held in captivity across a vast expanse of ocean, heightening her experience of loss and desperation. But there is hope! For Hanuman's wondrous leap across this "sea of separation" will set in motion the final acts of the epic, culminating in Ram's victory over his demonic adversaries and reunion with his beloved wife.

## *On the Translation*

The challenges inherent in rendering the *Mānas* in English have been noted before.[31] As a devotional work intended for episodic oral performance, the text seems repetitious when set in a linguistic medium that is normally experienced through individual, silent communion with the printed page, and its frequent use of formulaic phrases (though common in epic poetry worldwide) may appear redundant and saccharine—for example, "eyes filling with tears" and "limbs thrilling with love" (the latter, one choice for the nearly untranslatable *pulak*—in plain English, "goosebumps" or the dismally medical "horripilation"; besides "thrilling," I sometimes use "trembling," "quivering," "flushed," or "shivering"), and the poet's often-repeated assertion that some person, place, event, or emotion "cannot be described," which he usually follows with its very apt description. Some of Tulsi's apparent "repetitiveness," however, actually reflects the great asymmetry in lexicons between the two languages. English has more than one verb for "seeing"—the most important and recurrent act in which *Mānas* characters engage, especially "seeing" the unworldly beauty of Ram and Sita—but it does not have (as I have counted in *Bālkāṇḍ* alone) fourteen. Similarly, one can think of several synonyms for the adjective "beautiful" but not the twenty-two, each slightly different, that Tulsi deploys to convey the overwhelming visual attraction of his divine characters and their world. And, like "camel" in the Arabic lexicon, "lotus" in the *Mānas* is not a single word—rather, it is, by my count, twenty-nine, each nuanced and suited to different contexts of meaning, meter, rhyme, and alliteration. Tulsi's vocabulary is indeed immense, and he is often credited with having expanded the lexicon of what would become modern Hindi through his revival and adaptation of Sanskrit loanwords; no Sanskrit chauvinist, he also used, according to a recent count, more than ninety Arabic and

Persian ones.[32] In English, much of this verbal richness (to echo the poet) simply "cannot be expressed."

For the Murty Classical Library of India, my aim has been to produce a straightforward, readable, free-verse rendering in contemporary language. I readily concede that most of the enchanting music of Tulsidas—his rhyme, alliteration, and almost hypnotic rhythm—is lost in my version. What I seek to preserve, as much as possible, is clarity, compactness of expression, and a certain momentum.

*Acknowledgments*

I am grateful to Rohan Murty for his generosity and to the production staff of Harvard University Press for the extraordinary care and diligence they have brought to the production of this translation series. I thank general editor Sheldon Pollock and coeditor Francesca Orsini for offering me the opportunity to undertake this translation and for their subsequent guidance. I also thank the late Shrinath Mishra, a revered *rāmāyaṇī* (traditional *Mānas* scholar) of Banaras, for his generous help and encouragement, and Pranav Prakash for his careful editing and proofreading of the Devanagari text. Among early mentors who guided me toward this work, I gratefully cite the late Professors Emeritus Colin P. Masica and Kali Charan Bahl of the University of Chicago.

I dedicate this translation to Meher Baba, who inspires me; to the many *Mānas* scholars and devotees who have instructed and encouraged me; and to the memory of three dear mentors and friends—Ramji Pande, A. K. Ramanujan, and Chandradharprasad Narayan Singh ("Bhanuji").

## NOTES

1 For a more detailed general introduction to the *Mānas* and its author, see volume 1 of the Murty Classical Library translation, *The Epic of Ram* (Lutgendorf 2016: vol. 1, vii–xxii).

2 Macfie 1930; Growse 1978: xxxviii.

3 Gandhi 1968: 47; on the role of the *Mānas* in the emerging Hindi literary canon, see Orsini 1998.

4 McGregor 2003: 917–939.

5 *The Epic of Ram, Volume 1*, pp. 83–99; *Rāmcaritmānas* 1.36–43.

6 *The Epic of Ram, Volume 1*, p. 5; *Rāmcaritmānas* 1.0.7.

7 *The Epic of Ram, Volume 1; Rāmcaritmānas* 1.1–1.175.

8 *The Epic of Ram, Volume 2; Rāmcaritmānas* 1.176–1.361.

9 *The Epic of Ram, Volumes 3* and *4; Rāmcaritmānas* 2.1–2.326.

10 For discussion of such controversy, see Lutgendorf 1991: 392–407.

11 Lutgendorf 2007.

12 3.2–3 in Pollock 1991: 89–92; see *The Epic of Ram, Volume 3*, pp. 21–23 and *Rāmcaritmānas* 3.7.3–4.

13 3.57–61 in Pollock 1991: 211–223; see *The Epic of Ram, Volume 3*, p. 89 and *Rāmcaritmānas* 3.30.4–8.

14 *The Epic of Ram, Volume 3*, pp. 105–111; *Rāmcaritmānas* 3.37–38.

15 See *The Epic of Ram, Volume 1*, pp. 113–115 and *Rāmcaritmānas* 1.50.3–51.3; for further discussion, see Lutgendorf 1991: 355–356.

16 3.7.1–4 in Chhawchharia 2010: 1.336–337.

17 *The Epic of Ram, Volume 3*, pp. 69–71 and *Rāmcaritmānas* 3.23.4–24.3; see *The Epic of Ram, Volume 6*, pp. 261–265 and *Rāmcaritmānas* 6.108.7–109.

18 See *The Epic of Ram, Volume 2*, pp. 27–31 and *Rāmcaritmānas* 1.187–188.3

19 Lefeber 1994: 37–44.

20 *The Epic of Ram, Volume 3*, p. 139; *Rāmcaritmānas* 4.5.1.

21 Scholars of the *Vālmīki Rāmāyaṇa* have pointed out that the Sanskrit word *ṛkṣa*, which is now conventionally taken to mean "bear," originally referred to another species of anthropoid primate (for evidence, see Lefeber 1994: 38–39). However, by Tulsidas's time the members of this subgroup of allies were understood and also visually represented (in Mughal paintings, for example) as Himalayan bears, and it is clear that Tulsi visualized them thus.

22 See *Valmīki Rāmāyaṇa* 4.17–18 and the discussion of this episode in Lefeber 1994: 45–50, 87–95.

23 *The Epic of Ram, Volume 5*, p. 151; *Rāmcaritmānas* 4.9.2.

24 On the structure, emotional texture, and special destiny of the corresponding sub-book, *Sundarakāṇḍa*, in the *Vālmīki Rāmāyaṇa*, see Goldman and Goldman 1996, especially 13–37, 79–86.
25 Ibid., 75–78.
26 *The Epic of Ram, Volume 3*, pp. 231–233; *Rāmcaritmānas* 5.15.
27 *The Epic of Ram, Volume 3*, pp. 243–245; *Rāmcaritmānas* 5.21.2–21.
28 *The Epic of Ram, Volume 3*, p. 261 and *Rāmcaritmānas* 5.31.2–4; *The Sea of Separation*, p. 120 and *Rāmcaritmānas* 5.32.4.
29 *The Sea of Separation*, p.130; *Rāmcaritmānas* 5.43.
30 *The Sea of Separation*, p. 105; *Rāmcaritmānas* 5.14.1.
31 Growse 1978: lvii–lviii; Hill 1952: xx; Lutgendorf 1991: 29–33.
32 McGregor 2003: 938; Stasik 2009.

# *In the Forest*

To the root of dharma's tree, the full moon[1] 1
that gladdens and swells the sea of discernment,
glorious sun to the lotus of dispassion, wholly erasing
the darkness of amassed sins and triple torments,
sky-born wind that tears through massed clouds
of delusion—to Lord Shankar
I bow in homage, of Brahma's lineage
and destroyer of sin, who is dear to King Ram.[2]

And him—whose lovely body is like dark rain clouds 2
of bliss, who wears a glorious garment of yellow,
who holds in his two hands arrows and bow
and bears cinched at his waist an inexhaustible quiver,
whose eyes are like lotus petals, and whose forehead
is crowned by piled-up, matted locks,
who walks the path accompanied by Sita
and Lakshman—Ram, source of all delight, I adore.

Uma, Ram's nature is mysterious; learned ones 0
and sages gain detachment by contemplating it,
but fools who are averse to Lord Hari
and not devoted to dharma find only delusion.[3]

I have sung of the townsfolk and Bharat's love, 1
matchless and glorious, according to my understanding.
Now hear of the Lord's most purifying deeds
done in the forest, pleasing to gods, humans, and sages.
Once, when he had gathered lovely flowers, 2
with his own hands Ram crafted ornaments,
and with them, the Lord reverently adorned Sita

while seated on a beautiful crystalline rock.
3 Indra's son, Jayant, took on the guise of a crow,
for the rogue wanted to assay the Raghu's strength—
like a tiny ant before the ocean's abyss,
idiotically thinking to fathom it.
4 He pecked Sita's foot with his beak and fled,
that fool-turned-crow through moronic motive.
When blood flowed, the Raghu lord knew
and released from his bow an arrow of reed.[4]

1 The Raghu master is most merciful
and ever affectionate to the lowly,
yet that sin-ridden fool came
and tried to deceive him.

1 Inspired by mantra, the divine arrow raced
behind the fleeing, now frightened crow.
Assuming his own form, he went to his father,
but Indra would not shelter a foe of Ram.
2 He grew despondent, his mind filled with terror,
like Sage Durvasa menaced by the Lord's discus.[5]
Through Brahma's abode, Shiva's city, and all the worlds
he ranged, exhausted and undone by fear and anxiety,
3 yet no one even invited him to sit down,
for who can harbor an enemy of Ram?
His own mother becomes like death, his father, Yama,*
and—listen, Garuda—ambrosia turns to poison,[6]

* The god of death.

a friend does the misdeeds of a hundred foes, 4
the river of the gods turns into the Vaitarani,*
and the whole world gets hotter than an inferno
for one who turns against the Raghu hero, brother.
But when Narad saw Jayant's anguish, 5
he felt pity, for the holy are tenderhearted.
He sent him straightaway to Ram,
telling him to cry, "Benefactor of the meek, save me!"
Distraught and frightened, he went, clasped Ram's feet, 6
and cried, "Merciful Raghu king, save me! Save me!
Your strength and sovereignty are matchless,
but, being dull-witted, I could not grasp this.
I have gained the fruit of my own act, 7
but now save me, Lord, for I come seeking shelter!"
The merciful one heard his anguished speech
and let him go, Bhavani,† merely putting out one eye.[7]

In delusion's grip, he had acted in malice, 2
and though it would have been right to slay him,
the Lord showed pity and released him—
for who is as merciful as the Raghu hero?

Dwelling in Chitrakut, the Raghu lord 1
did countless deeds that are like nectar to the ears.[8]
But then Ram reasoned to himself,
"There will be crowds, for everyone knows me here."

---

* The river of hell.
† Parvati.

2 So, bidding farewell to the assembled sages,
and accompanied by Sita, the two brothers left.
When the Lord proceeded to Atri's ashram,
that great sage, hearing of it, was overjoyed.
3 His body thrilling with love, Atri arose and ran,
and Ram saw him and approached excitedly.
As he fell prostrate, the sage lifted and embraced him,
then bathed both brothers in tears of love.
4 The sight of Ram's beauty soothed his eyes
and he reverently brought him to his ashram.
Honoring and eloquently addressing him,
he offered roots and fruits that pleased the Lord's heart.

3 Gazing wide-eyed at the beauty of the Lord,
who was majestically seated there,
that great and supremely discerning sage
joined his palms and began a litany of praise.[9]

1 "I venerate you, who cherish your devotees,
who are by nature compassionate and tender.
I adore your lotus-like feet, that grant,
to those without desires, access to your abode.
2 Of a most beautiful, dark complexion,
you churn, like Mount Mandar, rebirth's sea,[10]
and, with eyes like full-bloomed lotuses,
liberate from pride and other sins.
3 The might of your long arms,
Lord, is as immeasurable as your glory.
Bearing a quiver, bow, and arrows,
you are sovereign of the three worlds,

ornament of the solar dynasty, 4
and breaker of the great god's[*] bow.
You delight eminent sages and holy ones,
and shatter the legions of the gods' foes.
Praised by the enemy of mind-born Kama,[†] 5
worshiped by unborn Brahma and all the gods—
to you, embodiment of pure enlightenment
and eradicator of all sins,
lordly husband of Indira,[‡] I bow in homage. 6
Wellspring of joy, haven of the holy, I praise you,
with your feminine power and junior brother—
yourself, dear younger brother of Shachi's lord.[11]
Those who cling to the soles of your holy feet 7
in adoration, spurning all jealous cravings,
do not fall into the ocean of rebirth
with its myriad waves of doubt.
Those who forever dwell in solitude, 8
joyfully worshiping you for liberation's sake,
aloof from all sensory desires,
attain the state of self-realization.
You are the unitary and marvelous Lord, 9
omnipresent God, beyond all desire,
world teacher and eternal one,
transcendent and utterly independent.[12]
I constantly adore you, who cherish loving feeling 10
and are unattainable by misguided yogis,[13]

* Shiva.
† Shiva.
‡ Lakshmi, wife of Vishnu.

but are a wish-granting tree to your devotees,
impartial to all and ever worthy of worship.
11 Incomparably beautiful ruler of the earth
and husband of her daughter*—I bow to you.
Be gracious to me—I salute you—
and grant me devotion to your holy feet.
12 Those who reverently recite this litany
of your praise attain the highest state
as well as devoted love for you—
of this there is no doubt!"[14]

4 The sage ended his prayer with bowed head,
and then, with palms joined, he added,
"Master, may my mind never stray
from the lake-born lotuses of your feet."

1 Then Sita touched the feet of Anusuya,†
meeting her with much courtesy and humility.
The seer's wife was greatly delighted
and, blessing her, made Sita sit beside her.
2 She dressed Sita in divine garments and jewelry
that would be ever lovely, fresh, and spotless,
and then that sage's spouse, in a sweet yet ardent voice,
used the occasion to expound some women's dharma.
3 "Mother, father, and brother are benefactors,[15]
but—listen, princess—these all give within limits.
He who gives limitlessly is a husband, Vaidehi,[16]

---

* Sita.
† Sage Atri's wife.

and a woman who does not serve him is contemptible.
Patience and righteousness, a friend, and a wife— 4
in times of distress, these four are tested.
He may be aged, sickly, stupid, or impoverished,
blind, deaf, prone to anger, or utterly wretched—
but if she shows disrespect to even such a husband, 5
a woman suffers countless torments in Yama's realm.[17]
A woman has but one duty, vow, and regimen:
to love with body, mind, and speech her husband's feet.
There are four kinds of faithful wives in this world,[18] 6
as the Veda, *purāṇas,* and holy ones all affirm.
In the heart of the highest kind abides the conviction
that, even in dreams, no other man exists on earth.
Those of middle rank look on another's husband 7
as if he were their own brother, father, or son.
Those who stay chaste thinking of duty and family honor
are low, third-rate women—so the sacred word declares—
and those who do so for lack of opportunity, or out of fear, 8
know to be the lowest of women in this world.
One who cheats her lord to make love to another
falls into the most dreadful hell for a hundred aeons.[19]
For a momentary pleasure, a billion lifetimes 9
of pain—who is so base that she cannot grasp this?
A woman effortlessly attains the supreme state
if she clings to the dharma of fidelity, giving up deceit.
But if she defies her husband, wherever she takes birth 10
she becomes a widow while still in her youth.

Though inherently impure, a woman 5a
gains salvation by serving her husband.

Praised in the four Vedas, the faithful Tulsi[20]
is even now beloved to Lord Hari.

5b But listen, Sita: merely recalling your name,
women will stay faithful to their husbands.
For you, Ram is dearer than life,
and I said all this only for the world's sake."

1 When she heard this, Janaki felt immense joy
and reverently bowed at Anusuya's feet.
Then Ram, abode of compassion, said to the sage,
"With your permission, we would go to another wood.
2 But please remain forever gracious to me,
and considering me your servant, be constant in affection."
To this speech by the Lord who upholds dharma,
that wise ascetic lovingly replied,
3 "You, whose grace Brahma, Shiva, Sanak and the sages,[21]
and all proponents of ultimate truth yearn to receive,
you alone, Ram—who cherish those without desire
and are brother to the poor—can speak so sweetly.
4 Now I truly grasp Shri's* cleverness
in adoring you, spurning all the other gods.[22]
One whom none can equal or surpass—
how could his nature be other than this?
5 And now, how can I say to you, 'Go, my lord'?
It is for you, master and inner knower, to say."
With this, that steadfast sage gazed at the Lord,
tears streaming from his eyes, his body thrilling.

* Lakshmi.

His body thrilling and filled with intense love, 6
he fixed his gaze on that lotus-like face, thinking,[23]
"For this sight of the Lord who transcends mind,
knowledge, attributes, and senses,
what meditation and austerity have I done?"
By mantra repetition, yoga, and adherence to all duties,
human beings attain incomparable devotion.
The blessed deeds of the Raghu hero
are sung, night and day, by his servant Tulsi.

Ram's glorious fame purges the Kali era's filth, 6a
subdues the mind, and is the root of joy,
and those who reverently listen to it
enjoy Ram's eternal favor.

This cruel age is a storehouse of sin, 6b
devoid of dharma, wisdom, yoga, and mantra repetition.
They alone who, abandoning all other hopes,
sing the praises of Ram are prudent ones.

After bowing his head at the sage's holy feet, 1
the God of gods, humans, and sages entered the forest.
Ram walked ahead, his younger brother behind,
both utterly charming in their ascetic garb,
and between the two, Shri* was as lovely 2
as divine illusion between *brahma* and the soul.[24]
Rivers, forests, mountains, and deep gorges,

* Lakshmi, but here, Sita.

recognizing their master, gave him clear passage,
3 and wherever the divine Raghu king walked,
clouds in the sky shaded those places.
Along the way, he encountered the demon Viradh,
whom the Raghu hero slew the moment he appeared.[25]
4 Viradh immediately obtained a glorious form,
and seeing him sorrowful, Ram sent him to his own abode.
Then to the abode of sage Sharabhang
Ram came, with his handsome brother and Janaki.

7 At the sight of Ram's lotus-like face,
the honeybees of the great sage's eyes
began to adoringly sip its nectar,
and Sharabhang's life was supremely blessed.

1 He said, "Hear my tale, merciful Raghu hero,
royal *haṃsa* on the Manas Lake of Shiva's heart:
I was leaving this world for Brahma's abode
when I heard that Ram would come to the forest.
2 Ever since, I have watched the path day and night,
and now, seeing my lord, my heart is appeased.
Though I lack all spiritual discipline, master,
you have shown me grace, recognizing a lowly devotee.
3 But, divine one, this was no special favor to me—
you only fulfilled your vow, thief of devotees' hearts![26]
Now, for this wretched one's sake, please remain here
until I relinquish this body and rejoin you."
4 All his yoga, rites, mantras, austerities, and fasts
he offered to the Lord, and received the boon of devotion.

Then sage Sharabhang built a pyre
and sat on it, purging his heart of all attachments,

saying, "My lord of cloud-dark limbs, 8
together with your younger brother and Sita,
reside eternally in my heart in the form
of Lord Ram, endowed with attributes!"

With this, he consumed his body in yogic fire 1
and went to Vaikunth by Ram's grace.
The sage was not merged in the Lord's infinitude,
for he had previously asked the boon of devotion-in-separation.[27]
The assembled seers witnessed the sage's exalted state 2
and greatly rejoiced in their hearts.
All those bands of ascetics sang his praises—
"Hail to the friend of refuge seekers, root of mercy!"
Then the Raghu lord went on through the forest 3
accompanied by many hosts of eminent sages.
Seeing a pile of human bones, the Raghu lord
felt great pity and questioned the sages, who replied,
"How is it that you ask us, Lord, when you already know, 4
for you are the all-seeing inner knower?
Hordes of night-stalkers* devoured all these sages."
When he heard, the Raghu hero's eyes grew moist.

Raising his arms, he said, "I solemnly vow 9
to rid the earth of night-stalkers!"

* Demons.

Then, one by one, he visited the ashrams
of all the sages and brought them joy.

1 There was a wise pupil of sage Agastya
named Sutikshan, who loved the supreme Lord.
Devoted to Ram's feet in thought, word, and deed,
he never dreamed of trusting in any other god.
2 When word of the Lord's coming reached his ears,
he ran forth, full of anxious yearning, and cried,
"Maker of fate, will the Raghu king, friend of the lowly
take pity on a scoundrel like me?
3 Will my master, Ram, along with his brother,
meet me like one of his very own servants?
My soul lacks steadfast faith,
my heart has no devotion, detachment, or wisdom.
4 I have not kept pious company, done yoga, mantra
 repetition, or fire rites,
and I lack firm attachment to his holy feet.
And yet, the treasury of mercy does have this trait:
those who rely on no other are dear to him.
5 Today these eyes of mine will achieve their goal,
seeing his lotus-like face that liberates from rebirth!"
Shiva observed, "The wise recluse was so immersed
in love, Bhavani, that his state cannot be described.
6 He lost all sense of direction on his path,
and awareness of himself or where he was going.
Sometimes he turned and went backward,
and sometimes danced, singing the Lord's praise.
7 As the sage attained profound loving devotion,
the Lord watched him, hidden behind a tree.

Perceiving his intense love, the Raghu hero,
who dispels rebirth's dread, appeared in his heart.
The sage became still and sat down on the path, 8
the hairs on his body erect as those on a jackfruit.
Then the Raghu lord approached him,
delighted at heart to see his servant's state.
Ram tried in many ways to rouse the sage, 9
but he would not awake from meditative bliss.
Thereupon, Ram concealed his regal, earthly form
and showed the sage's heart his four-armed one.
The sage then grew agitated and arose 10
like a desperate king cobra bereft of its jewel.[28]
There before him he beheld Ram's dark body—
abode of joy—along with Sita and his young brother.
Like a stick, he fell prostrate, clasping Ram's feet, 11
and that most fortunate sage was drowned in love.
Those long, dark arms grasped him, lifted him up,
and held him in a supremely loving embrace.
With the sage, the merciful Lord looked as lovely 12
as a dark evergreen enfolding a gold-hued tree.
Gazing at Ram's face, the recluse stood stock still
as if he were a figure drawn in a painting.

Then, composing his heart, the sage 10
repeatedly bowed to touch those holy feet,
and brought the Lord to his hermitage,
where he honored him in numerous ways.

The sage said, "Hear my prayer, Lord— 1
yet how may I sing your praise?

Your glory is limitless, and my meager intelligence
is like the flicker of a firefly facing the sun.
2 Your body dark as a garland of blue lotuses,
head crowned with matted locks, garbed as an ascetic,[29]
hands holding bow and arrows, quiver at your waist—
divine hero of the Raghu clan—I forever bow to you.
3 Like fire to burn the dense forest of delusion,
sun to nurture the clustered lotuses of holy ones,
lordly lion to the elephants of demon hosts,
and hawk to the fowl of rebirth—protect me always.
4 To you—with eyes red as lotuses and lovely attire,
night's sovereign* to the *cakor* birds of Sita's eyes,
wild gosling on the Manas Lake of Hara's† heart—
to you, Ram, of broad chest and long arms, I bow.
5 Like Garuda, you devour the snakes of doubt
and stifle the anguish born of stubborn reason.
Destroyer of rebirth, delight of divine hosts,
and treasury of mercy—protect me always.
6 Without attributes, yet possessing them, awful and gentle,
matchless one beyond knowledge, speech, and senses,
pure and utterly flawless, infinite one—
Ram, destroyer of earth's burden—I bow to you.
7 Grove of wish-granting trees for your devotees,
chastiser of anger, greed, arrogance, and lust,
supremely urbane one, causeway over rebirth's sea,
ensign of the solar lineage—protect me always.
8 Abode of strength, with incomparably mighty arms,

* The moon.
† Shiva.

whose name dissolves the Kali Age's amassed filth,
armor of dharma, endowed with delightful attributes—
Ram, enhance my felicity forever.
Though you are flawless, omnipresent, indestructible, 9
and eternally abide in the hearts of all beings,
yet, foe of Khar, with your brother and beloved wife,[30]
remain thus, as woodland wayfarers, in my heart!
Those with true knowledge, master—let them know you 10
as with and without attributes, the heart's inner knower.
But as for me, may he who is Kosala's lotus-eyed lord—
Ram—make his home in my heart,
and may I never, ever cease to feel pride[31] 11
in being a servant of the Raghu lord, my master!"
Ram was inwardly pleased by the sage's speech
and again joyfully embraced the noble ascetic, saying,
"Know me to be supremely satisfied, sage, 12
and whatever boon you ask, I will assuredly grant."
The sage replied, "I have never pleaded for a boon,
for I cannot even tell the true from the false.
Therefore, whatever seems good to you, Raghu king, 13
delight of your servants, give that to me."
Ram said, "Be a storehouse of profound devotion,
detachment, knowledge, and all virtues and wisdom."
"I have received my lord's own gift," said the sage, 14
"and now, grant me that for which I yearn—

accompanied by your brother and Janaki, lord, 11
may you, as bow and arrow-bearing Ram,
shine eternally, like the moon,
in the sky of my desireless heart."[32]

1 Saying, "It shall be so," Lakshmi's lord
left happily for the abode of pot-born Agastya.
But Sutikshan said, "I have not seen my guru
for a long time, since coming to this ashram.
2 If I now accompany you, lord, to my teacher,
it will put you under no obligation."[33]
The merciful one perceived the sage's ingenuity,
and both brothers laughed as they took him along.
3 Discoursing en route on the matchless merit of devotion,
the lord of gods reached the sage's ashram.
Sutikshan went at once to his guru,
prostrated fully at his feet, and said,
4 "Master, the son of Kosala's king
and support of the world has come to meet you
with his brother and Vaidehi—Ram,
holy one, whose name you repeat night and day!"
5 As soon as he heard this, Agastya arose and ran
to see Lord Hari, his eyes filled with tears.
Both brothers fell at the sage's holy feet
but, with great love, the seer drew them to his heart.
6 Politely inquiring of their well-being, that wise one
escorted them to comfortable seats.
Then, honoring the Lord in various ways,
he declared, "None is as fortunate as I am."
7 And all the other bands of sages residing there
were delighted to behold Ram, the root of bliss.

12 There he sat, in the midst of the sages,
face to face with them all,

and it was as though a flock of *cakor* birds
were gazing at the full moon of *śarad.*[34]

Then the Raghu hero said to the sage, 1
"Nothing can be hidden from you, lord.
You know the purpose for which I have come,
and so, revered one, I have not explained it.
Now give me sacred counsel, master,[35] 2
so that I may slay the sages' enemies."
The sage smiled to hear the Lord's words.
"What do you take me for, master, to ask of me?
Solely by virtue of worshiping you, destroyer of sin, 3
do I grasp even a little of your greatness.
Your cosmic illusion is a vast, wild fig tree[36]
with countless clusters of universes as its fruit.
All beings are like the miniscule creatures 4
who live inside them and know nothing beyond,
and the awful, inexorable devourer of those fruits—
eternally in dread of you alone—is fatal time.
And yet you, master of all lords of creation, 5
inquire of me like an ordinary man!
I ask this boon of you, abode of mercy:
abide in my heart, with Shri and your brother,
and grant me firm devotion, detachment, holy company, 6
and constant love for your lotus-like feet.
Although you are *brahma,* indivisible and eternal,
known only by experience and worshiped by the holy,
and I too understand and expound this as your reality, 7
yet I always come back to adoring you as embodied God.

You, for your part, forever exalt your servants,
which is why, Raghu king, you inquire of me.
8 There is a place, lord, that is most charming
and holy—its name is Panchavati.[37]
Purify the Dandak Forest, lord,
and lift the awful curse of the great sage.[38]
9 Make your abode there, Raghu king,
and show your mercy to all the ascetics."
At the sage's command, Ram went forth
and soon approached Panchavati.

13 He met with the vulture king,
greatly affirming their mutual love,[39]
and took up residence near the River Godavari,
after constructing a shelter of leaves.

1 From the time Ram made his abode there
the ascetics became happy and their fears passed.
Hills, forests, rivers, and ponds grew lovely,
with a beauty that increased with each day.
2 Flocks of birds and herds of animals lived blissfully
and honey-making bees buzzed sweetly.
Not even the thousand-tongued serpent could describe
that forest, wherein the Raghu hero manifested his glory.
3 Once when the Lord was seated contentedly,
Lakshman addressed him in great sincerity.[40]
"Lord of gods, humans, sages, and all beings—
I would inquire of you as my own master.
4 Explain to me, divine one, the means whereby
I may relinquish all to worship the dust of your feet.

Tell me of wisdom, detachment, illusion,
of the devotion that elicits your mercy,

and of the divide between God and the soul. 14
Explain all that to me, lord,
whereby intense love for your feet is gained
and sorrow, delusion, and error banished."

Ram replied, "I will explain it all, and in brief. 1
Listen, dear brother, with attentive understanding.
'I' and 'mine,' 'you' and 'your'—these are illusion,
which has brought all beings under its sway.
The senses and their objects, as far as the mind ranges— 2
know all that to be maya, brother,
and of its two varieties, hear the distinction:
one is knowledge and the other ignorance.
One is the evil embodiment of utter grief, 3
in whose grip souls fall into rebirth's abyss.
The other, which controls attributes, creates the world,
inspired by the Lord—not by any power of its own.
Knowledge arises where there is no trace of self-pride 4
and one sees *brahma* equally in all things.
One is called supremely detached, dear brother,
who spurns, like chaff, occult powers and the three
    qualities.[41]

The one who does not know maya, God, 15
or itself, is called the soul,
and the one who gives both bondage and release,
the transcendent one who incites maya, is God.[42]

1 From dharma arises detachment, from yoga, wisdom,
and wisdom grants liberation—so the Veda explains.
But that to which I quickly respond with favor, brother,
is devotion to me, which gives joy to my devotees.[43]
2 It is self-sufficient and depends on nothing else—
indeed, knowledge and wisdom depend on it.
Devotion, dear brother, is the matchless root of bliss,
obtained when the holy are favorable to one.
3 I will expound the means of cultivating devotion—
the easy path by which beings may attain me.
First, one should adore the feet of Brahman seers
and be intent on one's own work, as scripture prescribes.[44]
4 The fruit of this is detachment from sensual desires
and then, the birth of love for my own dharma.
'Listening' and other forms of ninefold devotion grow
firm,[45]
and fervent love for my playful acts pervades the heart.
5 One who adores the stainless feet of saintly ones,
resolutely worships me in thought, word, and deed,
and gives to guru, parents, brother, master, and gods[46]
devoted service, understanding them all to be me,
6 whose body thrills when singing of my virtues,
whose voice breaks and whose eyes shed tears,
and who is without lust, pride, hypocrisy and other vices—
to such a one, dear brother, I forever submit!

16 One devoted to me in word, deed, and thought,
who sings my praise without desire for reward—
within the heart-lotus of such a one
I continually rest contented."

Delighted by hearing of the yoga of devotion, 1
Lakshman bowed his head at his lord's feet.
Thus did many a day pass
amid talk of dispassion, wisdom, virtue, and ethics.
Now Ravan had a sister, Shurpanakha,[47] 2
wicked-hearted and fearsome as a serpent.
She came one day to Panchavati
and was smitten by the sight of the two princes.
For whether he be brother, father, or son—oh Garuda[48]— 3
when a woman spies a handsome man,
she grows distracted and cannot check her heart,
as a sunstone melts at the sight of the sun.[49]
Assuming a lovely form, she went to the Lord 4
and, with many a smile, declared,
"There is no other man like you, nor woman like me,
and fate has thoughtfully arranged our union.
In all creation, I have seen no man 5
fit for me, though I searched the three worlds.
Hence, till now, I have remained a virgin,
but I might change my mind, having seen you."
With a glance at Sita, the Lord said, 6
"My younger brother is a bachelor."[50]
She went to Lakshman, who knew her as their foe's sister
and, looking at the Lord, said politely,
"Listen, pretty one—I am but his servant 7
and dependent, and cannot provide for your comfort.
My lord is the almighty king of Kosala
and whatever he may do is fitting for him.[51]
A servant craving happiness; a beggar seeking honor; 8
a dissolute one, wealth; a libertine, salvation;

a covetous one, fame; and the haughty, life's four goals—
all such beings vainly seek to milk the sky!"[52]
9 So she turned and came back to Ram,
but the Lord again sent her to Lakshman,
who said at last, "He alone should wed you
who vows to renounce all sense of shame!"
10 Then she grew furious and went toward Ram,
revealing her own terrifying form.
When he saw Sita frightened, the Raghu lord
communicated with Lakshman by a sign.

17 With great deftness, Lakshman
sliced off her nose and ears,
as though sending, by his own hand,
a challenge to Ravan.

1 With nose and ears gone, she looked hideous,
like a mountain gushing streams of red ochre.
She went to Khar and Dushan, shrieking,[53]
"Shame on your virility and might, brothers!"
2 They questioned her, she explained it all,
and when they heard, the demons mustered their army.
Hordes of night-stalker legions came running,
like winged mountains of heaped-up soot,
3 with myriad vehicles and myriad forms,
toting myriad lethal weapons.
They placed Shurpanakha at their fore,
an earless, noseless ensign of inauspiciousness.
4 Countless fearful omens appeared,

but that doomed horde paid them no heed.
Roaring and swearing, they mounted the skies,
and beholding their army, each warrior exulted.
One said, "Capture the two brothers alive, 5
then kill them and carry off the woman!"
The whole sky became filled with dust,
and Ram summoned his brother and said,
"Take Janak's daughter to a cave in the hillside, 6
for a frightful night-stalker army has come.
Be alert!" When he heard the Lord's command,
Lakshman left, bow and arrows in hand, along with Shri.*
As he watched the enemy force approach, 7
Ram smiled and took up his immense bow.

He lifted his immense bow, and bound up 8
the matted locks on his head, looking as glorious
as if two cobras, on an emerald peak, were dueling
with a million streaks of lightning.[54]
Cinching a quiver at his waist, with his great arms
he seized his bow and, readying an arrow,
the Lord looked toward the foe, like a kingly lion
surveying a herd of bull elephants.

The phalanx of warriors charged forward 18
shouting, "Grab him! Seize him!"
like the demons who, seeing him all alone,
surround the young sun at dawn.[55]

* Sita, identified by an epithet of Lakshmi.

1 Beholding the Lord, they could not fire their arrows,
for that whole demon host was stupefied.
Khar and Dushan summoned their advisers and said,
"This prince is surely some jewel among men.
2 So many serpents, demons, gods, men, and sages
we have seen, conquered, and slain.
But truly, brothers, in all our lives,
we have never seen such beauty as his!
3 Though he mutilated our sister,
this matchless man should not be killed.
Just say, 'Quickly hand over that wife you hid,
and both you brothers can go home alive.'
4 Tell him I have said this,
and hurry back with his reply."
The emissaries went and spoke to Ram,
and when he heard them, he smiled and said,
5 "We are Kshatriyas, hunting game in the forest
and searching for nasty beasts of your ilk.
Seeing a powerful foe, we are unafraid
and will duel with Death himself, if he comes.
6 Though we are men, we destroy the demon race,
and though young, protect sages and punish sinners.
If you lack strength, then go back home,
for I never strike anyone who turns away from war.
7 But once battle is joined, guile, subterfuge,
and mercy to a foe are the height of cowardice!"
The messengers hurried back to report all this,
and hearing it, Khar and Dushan blazed with rage.

Their hearts ablaze with rage, they cried, "Seize him!" 8
as ferocious night-stalker troops raced forward
bearing bows and arrows, javelins, pikes,
spears, sabers, sickles, and battle-axes.[56]
But the Lord first made his bowstring twang
with a sound so deep and terrifying
that the demons were deafened and bewildered
and, in that moment, completely lost their wits.

Then they advanced more warily, 19a
knowing their foe to be powerful,
and began to shower Ram
with all kinds of deadly arms.

The Raghu hero pulverized their weapons 19b
as though they were sesame seeds,
and then, stretching the bowstring to his ear,
let loose his own arrows.

Then those awful arrows sped forth, 1
hissing like a mass of king cobras.[57]
Lord Ram, angered on the field of war,
released his razor-sharp arrows.
At the sight of their honed blades 2
the demon stalwarts turned and fled.
The three brothers were enraged[58]
and said, "Whoever runs from the field
we will slay with our own hands!" 3
So they went back, resolved to die,

and unleashed a barrage of weapons
of all kinds, directly facing their foe.
4 Knowing the enemy was greatly aroused,
the Lord reset his bow, took aim,
and released a swarm of iron-tipped arrows[59]
that began slicing into the monstrous demons.
5 Trunks, heads, arms, hands, and feet
were falling to the ground on all sides.
The demons shrieked with the arrows' impact
and their mountain-like bodies toppled.
6 But though cut in hundreds of pieces
the fighters got up again by wizardry.
Severed arms and heads flew in the sky
and decapitated bodies ran about,
7 as vultures, crows, and jackals
made dreadful chomping noises.

8 Jackals' teeth chomped as ghosts, ghouls,
and goblins filled up cranial cups,
vampiric spirits beat out a rhythm
on warriors' skulls while *joginīs* danced.[60]
The Raghu hero's ferocious arrows sliced into
the chests, arms, and heads of combatants,
and their trunks fell everywhere, but then arose
to fight anew, with dreadful cries of "Grab him! Get him!"

9 Seizing entrails, vultures flew off
while ghouls held their other ends and raced about,
so that these denizens of the city of war
seemed like a bunch of children flying kites.

Struck and thrown down, their chests rent,
countless warriors lay groaning.
Seeing their army in distress, the champions
Trishira, Khar, and Dushan turned to face Ram.

Arrows, spears, lances, axes, tridents, 10
and daggers, all in a volley,
were furiously hurled at the Raghu hero
by countless rangers of the night.
In an instant, the Lord evaded his foes' arrows
and challenged them, releasing his own,
and sinking ten arrows each into the breasts
of every one of the demon commanders.

Those champions fell to earth, then rose to fight again, 11
undying through the potent working of their magic,
and the gods grew fearful, seeing fourteen thousand
evil spirits arrayed against the one lord of Avadh.
When he perceived that gods and sages were afraid,
the master of maya performed a great wonder:
seeing one another as Ram and engaging in combat,
the enemy army fought and died.

Shouting, "Ram! Ram!" they shed their bodies 20a
and attained a liberated state.[61]
By this means, the treasury of mercy
slaughtered his foes in an instant.

The gods, overjoyed, rained down blossoms 20b
as their celestial kettledrums resounded.

Then, uttering hymns of praise, they all departed,
resplendent on their many vehicles.

1 When the Raghu lord triumphed over his foes in battle,
the terror of gods, humans, and sages was ended
and Lakshman brought Sita back.
Falling at their lord's feet, they were lifted in his joyful
embrace.
2 Sita gazed at his dark and delicate form
with supreme love, her eyes ever unsated.
Thus the lord of Raghus dwelt in Panchavati
doing deeds that delighted gods and sages.
3 When she saw the annihilation of Khar and Dushan,[62]
Shurpanakha went off to incite Ravan
and spoke to him in great anger:
"Heedless of the welfare of your lands and holdings,
4 you guzzle drink and doze off, day and night,
unaware that a foe is lording it over you!
Kingship without statecraft, wealth without dharma,
good deeds that are not offered to Lord Hari,[63]
5 knowledge without the cultivation of discernment—
the study, practice, and gain of these is futile labor.
An ascetic, through attachment; a king, by bad advice;
wisdom by arrogance; modesty by drunkenness;
6 love by lack of respect; and a virtuous one, by pride:
all soon come to ruin—such counsel I have heard.

21a An enemy, an illness, fire, sin, a master,
or a snake should never be underestimated!"

Lamenting thus in various ways,
Shurpanakha began to wail loudly.

There in the court she collapsed in anguish, 21b
crying again and again,
"While you are alive, ten-necked lord,
how can I be brought to such a state?"

At this, the courtiers arose in distress 1
and lifted up Shurpanakha, consoling her.
The lord of Lanka said, "Tell your story—
who has deprived you of nose and ears?"
She replied, "The sons of Dasarath, king of Avadh, 2
lion-like men, came to hunt in the forest.
By their deeds, I came to understand
that they would rid the earth of night-rangers,
and by the protection of their arms, ten-headed one, 3
sages now wander the woods unafraid.
They look to be youths, but are like Death himself—
resolute, master bowmen of countless virtues.
Incomparably strong and energetic, both brothers 4
diligently slay evildoers and gladden gods and sages.
One, named 'Ram,' is the epitome of comeliness,
and with him is a most lovely young woman[64]
whom the creator crafted as such a treasury of beauty 5
that a billion Ratis* would die for her looks!
His younger brother cut off my ears and nose,

* The wife of Kama, god of love.

and hearing I was your sister, they mocked me.
6 When Khar and Dushan responded to my cries
he slaughtered their entire army in an instant."
Hearing of the slaying of Khar, Dushan, and Trishira,
ten-headed Ravan's whole body burned with rage.

22 He reassured Shurpanakha
with much boasting of his own strength,
but went to his abode deeply anxious
and could not sleep a wink that night, thinking,

1 "Among gods, men, demons, divine serpents and birds,
there is none to equal even my lackeys,
and Khar and Dushan were as powerful as I am,
so who could kill them but the Lord himself?
2 The pleaser of gods and breaker of earth's burden—
if that blessed one has taken form as avatar,
then I will go and resolutely oppose him,
give up my breath by God's arrows, and escape rebirth.
3 Devotion is impossible in this base form of mine,[65]
so this is sound counsel for my thought, speech, and act.
And if they are merely some human king's sons,
I'll defeat the two in battle and make off with the woman."
4 He mounted his chariot and went, all alone,
to where Marich was living, on the ocean's shore.
"Meanwhile," Shiva said, "of Ram's own stratagem
you must hear, Uma, for it is a delightful tale."[66]

23 When Lakshman went into the forest
to collect wild roots, fruits, and tubers,

the treasury of mercy and bliss spoke
with a smile to Janak's daughter:

"Dear one, devoted to your vows, and most virtuous— 1
listen: I will soon enact a beguiling human play.
Go and abide in the midst of purifying fire
while I annihilate the night-roaming demons."
Ram had no sooner explained all this 2
than she placed his feet in her heart and entered the fire.
But Sita left her own likeness there,
of exactly the same character, beauty, and modesty.
Not even Lakshman knew the secret 3
of this act that the blessed Lord had contrived.
Ten-faced Ravan went to where Marich dwelt
and bowed politely, though he was self-interested and vile.
For when the base abase themselves, much grief ensues, 4
as from the bending of a goad, bow, snake, or cat,[67]
and sweet talk from scoundrels is as alarming
as flowers blooming out of season, Bhavani.

Then Marich duly honored him 24
and politely inquired:
"My son,* why is your mind so perturbed
that you have come here all alone?"

Ten-faced Ravan put before him the whole story— 1
that ill-fated wretch—with haughty bluster,
and said, "Turn into a deceptive, magical deer

* Marich is Ravan's uncle.

so I may snatch away the prince's wife."
2 But Marich replied, "Listen, lord of ten heads—
he is Supreme Lord of all beings, in human guise.
Do not oppose him, my son,
for one dies or lives solely at his whim.[68]
3 When these princes went to guard the sage's rite,
the Raghu lord struck me with a headless arrow
and I was carried a hundred leagues in an instant.[69]
No good will come from antagonizing him.
4 Now I am like an insect seized by a predatory wasp[70]
and wherever I look, I see those two brothers!
Even if he is merely human, son, he is a great warrior
and you will never succeed by opposing him.

25 He who slew Taraka and Subahu,
who shattered Hara's bow,
and slaughtered Khar, Dushan, and Trishira—
can such a mighty one be a mere man?

1 Go home, mindful of the welfare of your clan!"
At this, Ravan flared up and showered him with abuse:
"Imbecile! Like a guru, you want to enlighten me,
but tell me: what warrior in the world is my equal?"
2 Then Marich pondered in his heart—
"There are nine whom it is best not to oppose:
an armed man, one privy to your secrets, a master, a fool,
a rich man, physician, genealogist, poet, or clever cook."[71]
3 Seeing that he was doomed either way,
he set his sight on the shelter of the Raghu king,
and thought, "If I talk back, this wretch will slay me,

so why not die by the Raghu lord's arrow?"
This certainty in his heart, he went with Ravan, 4
his love firmly focused on Ram's feet.
Though he did not reveal it, his heart rejoiced:
"Today I will behold my most dear one.

Beholding my supremely beloved one, 5
my eyes will be rewarded and I will find joy.
Accompanied by Shri and his young brother,
he is mercy's abode, at whose feet I will lay my heart.
He whose wrath gives release, and who,
though wholly independent, is swayed by devotion,[72]
with his own hands, will take aim with an arrow,
and then, Lord Hari, sea of bliss, will slay me.

He will be chasing me, intent on my capture, 26
bearing his arrows and bow—in this way,
turning my head time and again, I will see the Lord.
No, none is as blessed as I am!"

As ten-headed Ravan approached that forest, 1
Marich became an illusory deer,
most extraordinary and indescribable,
with a golden body studded with jewels.
Sita beheld that most pleasing animal, 2
its every limb enchantingly embellished,
and said, "Divine one, merciful Raghu hero,
this deer has an exceedingly lovely pelt.
Slay it, my lord who is faithful to his vows,[73] 3
and bring me its hide." So Vaidehi spoke,

and the Raghu lord, who knew the whole secret,
rose joyfully to attend to the task of the gods.
4 Marking the deer, he cinched his waistcloth,
took up his bow, and affixed a fine arrow.
Then the Lord instructed Lakshman:
"Many night-stalkers roam this forest, brother,
5 so guard Sita diligently, with intelligence
and strength, mindful of the situation."
Looking at Ram, the deer bounded off
and Ram ran after it, readying bow and arrow.
6 He—of whom Veda says, "Not this," whom Shiva's
meditation
cannot fathom—chased after an illusory deer!
Sometimes coming close, then dashing off,
at times showing, at times concealing himself, the deer
7 appeared and disappeared with great cunning,
and so he led the Lord far afield.
Then, taking aim, Ram fired a mighty arrow
and the deer fell to earth with a loud cry.
8 First he called out Lakshman's name,
and then inwardly meditated on Ram.
Giving up his life, he resumed his own form
and recalled Ram with deep affection.
9 The all-knowing Lord recognized his inner love
and gave him the state that eludes even sages.

27 Releasing a torrent of blossoms, the gods
sang the glory of the Lord:
"The Raghu master, friend of the lowly,
gave his own supreme state to a demon!"

The villain slain, the Raghu hero quickly turned back, 1
looking splendid with bow in hand, quiver at his waist.
But when Sita heard the deer's anguished cry,
she grew most frightened and said to Lakshman,
"Go at once, for your brother is in grave peril!" 2
Lakshman merely smiled, and said, "Listen, mother:
the mere arch of his brow wreaks cosmic destruction—
so can he, even in a dream, be imperiled?"
But when Sita spoke stinging words,[74] 3
at the Lord's instigation, Lakshman's mind wavered.
Entrusting her to the gods of the forest and directions,
he went to the Rahu* who devours Ravan's moon.
At this moment, seeing her alone, ten-necked Ravan 4
approached in the guise of an ascetic.
He—fear of whom so frightened gods and titans
that they could neither sleep at night nor eat by day—
that ten-headed one, like a stealthy dog, 5
came bent on thievery, glancing this way and that.
"King of birds," said Bhushundi, "one who thus sets foot
on an evil path loses all luster, wit, and bodily strength!"[75]
Addressing Sita, he concocted all sorts of pretty fables 6
displaying stratagem, threats, and allurement.
Sita answered, "Pardon me, revered ascetic,
but you have spoken like a wicked man."
Then Ravan revealed to her his true shape, 7
and when he told her his name she grew afraid.
But Sita summoned all her courage to say,
"Stand still, villain, for my lord approaches.

* The eclipse demon, but here, Ram.

8 Like a measly rabbit hankering for a lion's mate,
you are in death's grip, night-stalker king!"
When he heard this, the ten-headed one was enraged,
yet inwardly he bowed at her feet and was pleased.[76]

28 Then, seething with anger, Ravan
seized her, seated her in his chariot,
and anxiously took to the sky,
too fearful to urge on his steeds.

1 Sita cried, "Alas! Raghu king, earth's singular champion!
For what sin of mine have you forgotten your mercy?
Dispeller of affliction, delight of refuge seekers,
sun to the lotuses of the Raghu line—alas!
2 Alas, Lakshman, you were not at fault,
and I reap the fruit of my anger at you!"
Thus Vaidehi greatly lamented:
"My most merciful, loving lord is far away
3 and who will tell him of my peril?
Alas, an ass wants to eat the gods' portion!"[77]
When they heard Sita's piteous cries,
all created beings were grief stricken.
4 Hearing that cry of distress, the vulture king
knew that the wife of the best of Raghus
was being carried off by a vile night-stalker,
like a tawny cow seized by a barbarian.
5 Jatayu said, "Sita, my daughter, do not fear,
for I will destroy this demon!"
Enraged, the great bird swooped down
like a thunderbolt falling on a mountain.

"You scoundrel, you—halt and stand! 6
You brazenly flee, but do you not know me?"
Seeing him approach like Death himself,
ten-necked Ravan turned to assess him.
"Can this be Mount Mainak, or the king of birds?[78] 7
But no—he and his master already know my might."
Then he realized, "Why, it is old Jatayu,
come to shed his body at the shrine of my hands!"
At this, the vulture swooped down in a rage 8
saying, "Listen to my advice, Ravan.
Release Janak's daughter and go safely home,
or else, many-armed one, it will come to pass
that in the awful inferno of Ram's rage 9
your entire clan will burn like locusts!"
When the ten-faced warrior gave no reply,
the vulture rushed at him in fury
and, seizing him by the hair, threw him to the ground. 10
Then, setting Sita down, the bird turned again
and attacked with his beak, tearing into Ravan's flesh
so that he fainted for a time.
Then, in a fit of rage, the night-stalker 11
unsheathed his most terrible sword
and severed the bird's wings, so that he fell to earth,
remembering Ram and his wondrous deeds.[79]
Then Ravan put Sita back in his chariot 12
and sped off, more than a little frightened.
Sita wailed as she went through the sky,
like a terrified doe ensnared by a hunter.
Seeing some monkeys seated on a hill, 13
she said the Lord's name and threw down a garment.

And so that wicked one carried off Sita
and secured her in his grove of *aśoka* trees.[80]

29a When, despite all his blandishments and threats,
the villain was utterly frustrated,
he left her beneath an *aśoka* tree,
having made suitable arrangements.[81]

29b The graceful manner in which Lord Ram
had run off in pursuit of the false deer—
this Sita held firmly in her heart,
and continuously repeated the Lord's name.

1 When the Raghu lord saw his brother approach
he outwardly displayed great anxiety—
"Leaving Janak's daughter all alone,
you come, brother, setting aside my order!
2 Night-stalker bands roam this forest,
and my heart doubts that Sita is in our ashram."
Falling at his feet, his brother saluted him,
saying, "Master, it was no fault of mine!"
3 Then the Lord and his brother went
to where the ashram stood on Godavari's bank,
and when he saw it without Sita,
he grew distraught and wretched, like a worldly man.
4 "Alas for Sita, Janak's daughter, treasury of virtues,
of purest beauty, character, restraint, and discipline!"
Lakshman tried in many ways to console him
as he roamed about, asking trees and creepers:
5 "You birds, beasts, and lines of honeybees—

have you seen my doe-eyed Sita?[82]
The wagtail, parrot, dove, deer, and fish,
the bee swarm and sweet-voiced cuckoo,
jasmine and pomegranate, a flash of lightning, 6
autumn's lotuses and moon, a lustrous black snake,
Varuna's snare, Kama's bow, the *haṃsa* bird,
elephant, and lion—all can now hear their own praise.
Wood apple, gold, and plantain tree rejoice, 7
their hearts purged of doubt and shyness.
Today, Janaki, with you gone,
they are all as happy as if they had won kingdoms.
But how can you suffer this peeved jealousy, 8
darling? Why not show yourself at once?"
So her lord lamented as he frantically searched,
like a lustful, worldly person crazed by separation.
Though Ram is the all-sufficient treasury of bliss, 9
unborn and imperishable, he acted as an ordinary man.
Advancing, he saw the fallen vulture king,
meditating on Ram's feet and their sacred marks.[83]

The Raghu hero, ocean of mercy, 30
laid his lotus-like hand on his head,
and seeing Ram's face, abode of beauty,
all Jatayu's pain vanished.

Then the great bird composed himself and spoke: 1
"Oh Ram, destroyer of the agonies of rebirth,
the ten-faced one has done this to me.
That scoundrel kidnapped Janak's daughter
and carried her off to the south, master, 2

while she wailed like a frightened curlew.[84]
I have clung to my breath to see you, lord,
but now, abode of mercy, it yearns to depart."
3 Ram said, "Keep your body, revered friend!"
But the bird smiled and spoke these words:
"When he—whose name, uttered at the moment of death,
liberates even vile ones, as the Veda declares—
4 when that very one stands before my eyes,
for want of what, master, would I cling to this body?"
With tears in his eyes, the Raghu lord said,
"Noble one, by your deeds you have won salvation,
5 for to one who cherishes the welfare of others,
nothing in this world is unattainable.
Quit your body, friend, and go to my abode.[85]
What can I give you, who are utterly fulfilled?

31 But of Sita's abduction, dear friend, do not
speak to my father when you get there.
For if I am truly Ram, the ten-faced one himself,
together with his clan, will come and tell him."

1 The vulture shed his form and took that of Lord Hari,
with many ornaments, matchless saffron-hued garment,
and a dark body with four mighty arms,
and, eyes brimming with tears, uttered this hymn:[86]

2 "Hail to you, Ram, of incomparable beauty, formless
and with form, sole instigator of all attributes.
You bear angry arrows to sever the mighty arms
of ten-headed Ravan, and are earth's ornament,

with cloud-dark body, lotus-like face,
and eyes like large, full blooming lotuses.
I ever adore you, compassionate Ram,
long-armed liberator from rebirth's dread.

Of immeasurable might, beginningless, unborn, 3
invisible, unitary, imperceptible to the senses,
lord of the senses and yet beyond them, remover
of dualities, dense mass of wisdom, earth's bearer—
you delight the hearts of saintly ones who repeat
the Ram mantra, and of myriad devotees.
I forever worship Ram, to whom the desireless are dear,[87]
and who defeats the legions of lust and sin.

He whom the sacred word hails as transcendent *brahma,* 4
calling him omnipresent, stainless, and unborn,
and whom by practice of meditation, knowledge,
detachment, and yoga countless sages have attained,
he is a cloud of compassion, manifest as a treasury
of beauty to enchant inert and sentient beings,
and as a bee on the mud-born lotus of my heart,[88]
his every limb gleaming with the luster of countless
Kamas.

He who is unattainable and yet accessible, innately pure, 5
terrible and benign, and eternally serene,
who is perceived by yogis only through great effort
and constant control over their minds and senses—
Ram, Lakshmi's beloved lord, and master[89]
of the three worlds, ever mastered by his servants,

may he abide in my heart—he whose purest renown
quells the tumultuous cycle of rebirth."

32 Asking the boon of profound devotion,
the great vulture left for Hari's abode,
and his last rites were fittingly performed,
with his own hands, by Lord Ram.

1 That most tenderhearted benefactor of the poor,
the causelessly compassionate Raghu Lord,
gave to a vulture—a vile flesh-eating bird—
the state for which great yogis plead.
2 Shiva observed, "How unfortunate are those, Uma,
who spurn Hari to lust after sensual pleasures!"
Then the two brothers, again searching for Sita,
moved on, looking through dense forest
3 thick with vines and masses of trees
and full of birds, deer, elephants, and lions.
Along the way, they struck down Kabandh,
and then he told them all about his curse.[90]
4 "Sage Durvasa had cursed me,
but seeing your feet, lord, that sin of mine is erased."
Ram said, "Hear what I say, heavenly minstrel:
No foe of Brahmans is pleasing to me.

33 Abandoning hypocrisy in thought, act, and word,
one who humbly serves the gods of this earth
comes to command all deities, including
Brahma and Shiva, as well as me.

Though he curses or strikes you, or speaks harshly, 1
a seer merits homage—so the holy declare.
Even without propriety and virtue, a Brahman deserves worship,
but not a Shudra, however meritorious and learned."
Thus Ram expounded his own dharma to Kabandh, 2
and seeing his humble devotion, gratified his heart.
Bowing his head at the Raghu lord's pure feet,
he regained his own form and rose to the sky.
Having liberated Kabandh, beneficent Ram 3
proceeded to the ashram of Shabari.
When Shabari saw Ram enter her home
she recalled the sage's words and was delighted.[91]
With their lotus-like eyes and long arms, 4
heads crowned with matted locks, wearing wildflower garlands,
the two brothers, dark and fair, were most lovely,
and Shabari fell and clung to their feet.
Immersed in love, unable to speak, 5
she bowed, again and again, at those holy feet,
then reverently brought water to wash them
and escorted the brothers to comfortable seats.

Then, bringing roots and tubers 34
and the juiciest fruits, she gave them to Ram,
and the Lord lovingly ate them,
praising them again and again.

She stood before him, palms reverently joined, 1
gazing at the Lord with ever-growing love.

"How may I voice your praise,
being of vile birth, very foolish,
2 the lowest of the low, and lower still—a woman—
and among them, too, dull-witted, oh destroyer of sin?"
The Raghu lord said, "Listen to me, good woman:
I esteem but one relationship—devotion.
3 Caste status and kinship, piety, renown,
wealth, power, lineage, virtues, and cleverness—
a person with all of these, yet without devotion,
seems as arid as a cloud without rainwater.
4 I will tell you devotion's ninefold practice,
so listen attentively and set it in your heart.
The first is keeping the company of the holy,
the second is love for the events of my story.[92]

35 Selfless service at a guru's holy feet
is the third way of devotion,
and the fourth is to abandon hypocrisy
and sing the litany of my praise.

1 Firm faith in repeating my mantra
is the fifth practice, revealed in the Veda.
The sixth: sense control and detachment in all tasks,
with constant adherence to the dharma of the good.
2 The seventh is to see all creation imbued with me
and to hold the holy above even myself.
The eighth is to be content with one's lot
and to not even dream of seeing others' faults.
3 The ninth is simplicity and honesty toward all,
with heartfelt trust in me, regardless of joy or woe.

Practicing even one of these nine,
any being—female or male, animate or inert—
is exceedingly dear to me, good woman, 4
and in you all forms of devotion are firm-rooted.
And so, the blessed state that eludes even yogis
has today become easy for you to reach.
For the matchless, supreme fruit of seeing me 5
is the soul's attainment of its own innate nature.
But if, good lady, you know of any news
of King Janak's lovely daughter, then tell me."[93]
She replied, "Raghu king, go to Lake Pampa, 6
where you will make friends with Sugriv.
He will tell you all, divine Raghu hero,
as you well know, though you patiently ask of me."
Laying her head again and again at the Lord's feet, 7
she related her whole story with great love.[94]

Relating her whole tale, gazing at Lord Hari's face, 8
she placed his pure feet in her heart
and shed her body in yogic flames, to be merged
in the Lord's feet, whence there is no return.
Oh people! Abandon all actions, immorality,
and false doctrines that yield only sorrow,
and with faith—says servant Tulsi—
cultivate fervent love for Ram's feet.

To such a woman—bereft of caste status, 36
and the very womb of sin—he gave liberation.
And yet, stupid mind, you seek happiness
in forgetting such a Lord!

1 Leaving that wood, Ram proceeded with his brother—
both incomparably strong, lions among men.
The Lord lamented like any separated lover,
recounting many stories and conversations.
2 "Look, Lakshman, at the beauty of the forest—
seeing it, whose mind would not be disturbed?
Joined with their mates, all the birds and animals
seem as if they are mocking me.
3 When they see us, deer herds scatter,
but their does say to them, 'Do not fear!
Be at ease, for you are born of ordinary deer
and these men come in search of a golden one.'
4 The elephant bulls keep their cows close by,
as though teaching me a lesson:
even a well-known text must be constantly reviewed,
a well-served king must not be taken for granted,
5 nor a wife, however firmly held in one's heart—
for a young woman, text, and king cannot be mastered!
Look, brother, at the glory of springtime—
yet without my beloved, it awakens dread in me.

37a Reckoning me distracted by separation,
powerless and utterly alone,
love-god Madan* has mustered forests,
bees, and birds to mount an assault.

37b But when his spy, seeing my brother with me,
went back to him and he heard this report,

* Kama.

it seems the mind-born god halted his legions
and made camp.

These huge trees overspread with vines 1
are like the many tents they have pitched.
Plantains and palms are their lofty standards,
captivating anyone who lacks a resolute mind.
Countless trees bear every kind of blossom, 2
like warriors arrayed in varied uniforms.
Here and there, lovely scattered trees
are like soldiers who have pitched solitary camps.
Cuckoos cry like aroused bull elephants, 3
*ḍhek* and *mahokh* birds bray like camels and donkeys.[95]
Peacocks, *cakors,* parrots, pigeons, and *haṃsas*
all are like fine Arabian horses,
quail and partridge are legions of foot soldiers— 4
but the mind-born god's army is beyond description!
High cliffs are his chariots, waterfalls his war drums,
and the sparrow hawk his bard, reciting his praise.
Noisy bees sound his drums and reed pipes 5
and a cool, fragrant breeze arrives as his emissary.
And so, equipped with his fourfold army,[96]
he ambles forth, boldly challenging everyone.
Lakshman, beholding Kama's horde, only one 6
who can stand firm deserves the world's esteem.
His ultimate weapon is woman,
and only he who escapes her is a true warrior.

Brother, the three mightiest villains 38a
are lust, anger, and greed,

which in an instant can perturb
the minds of even the wisest sages.

38b Greed is empowered by desire and arrogance,
lust, solely by woman,
and anger by harsh speech—
so great sages, having pondered, declare."

1 Shiva said, "Beyond attributes, master of all beings—
Ram is the inner knower of all, Uma.
But he revealed the wretchedness of the lustful
to strengthen detachment in steadfast ones' hearts.
2 Anger, lust, greed, arrogance, and illusion
are all relinquished through Ram's mercy,
and one will not stray into the web of magic
who has found favor with that conjurer.[97]
3 Uma, I say from my own experience:
Hari's worship alone is real; this whole world, a dream."
Then the Lord went to the shore of the lake
named Pampa, beautiful and deep,
4 its water clear as the hearts of holy ones,
and bounded by four charming embankments.
On all sides, diverse animals drank of its water,
like mendicants flocking to a generous home.

39a Lotus pads so densely covered it
that its water could not at first be perceived,
just as, behind the screen of maya,
God beyond attributes remains invisible.

Fish all lived in constant delight 39b
in the lake's profound depths,
as those who adhere to dharma
pass their days in happiness.

Lotuses of many hues bloomed there 1
and countless bees buzzed sweetly.
Waterfowl and noble *haṃsas* called out
as if, seeing the Lord, they broke into praise.
The multitude of geese, herons, and other birds 2
was indescribable unless actually seen.
In sweet voices, these flocks of lovely fowl
seemed to call out to passing wayfarers.
Near the lake, sages had made their abodes, 3
surrounded by majestic forest trees—
*campak, bakul, kadamb,* evergreen *tamāl,*
trumpet flower, jackfruit, flame of the forest, mango—
countless trees, bearing new leaves and blossoms 4
above which swarms of bees hummed.
Naturally cool, gentle, and fragrant,
an enchanting breeze always blew there.
Cuckoos cried, "*Kuhū, kuhū,*" 5
and the sweet sound disturbed sages' concentration.

Laden with fruit, all the trees 40
are bent near to the earth,
as benevolent people are humbled
by acquiring great wealth.

1 When Ram beheld this most beautiful lake,
he bathed in it and felt immense joy,
and in the shade of a noble tree
the Raghu lord and his brother sat down.
2 Then all the gods and sages came once more,
lauded him, and returned to their abodes.
Sitting there, supremely content, the merciful one
recounted charming tales to his younger brother.
3 To see the Lord suffering in separation,
Sage Narad grew especially troubled at heart.[98]
"By accepting my curse,
Ram bears the weight of countless sorrows.[99]
4 Let me go to behold such a Lord,
for a chance like this may not come again."
Reflecting thus, Narad took up his vina
and went to where the Lord was contentedly seated,
5 singing of Ram's noble deeds in a sweet voice
and praising him with love in diverse ways.
When he prostrated himself, Ram drew him up
and held him to his breast for a long time.
6 Greeting him politely, he seated him by his side
while Lakshman reverently washed the sage's feet.

41 After making many entreaties,
and knowing the Lord's heart to be pleased,
Narad joined his lovely palms in supplication
and spoke these words—

1 "Naturally bounteous Raghu lord, hear me:
you bestow favors, both difficult and easy.

I beseech you to grant me one, master,
though you already know it in your omniscience."
Ram said, "Sage, you know my nature. 2
Do I ever withhold anything from my people?
What could ever seem so dear to me
that you, best of sages, cannot ask for it?
I have nothing that I would not give to my servants— 3
never, ever lose your faith in this!"
Then Narad spoke joyfully,
"Just such a boon I would audaciously ask:
Though God has so many names, 4
and sacred lore declares each highly laudable,
let the name 'Ram' surpass all others,
master, as a fowler to snare the birds of sin.

On the full-moon night of devotion to you, 42a
let the name 'Ram' be the glorious moon,
and other names, the gleaming host of stars
shining in the firmament of devotees' hearts."

"So it shall be, sage," 42b
said the Raghu master, sea of mercy,
and then Narad, his heart overjoyed,
bowed his head at the Lord's feet.

Knowing the Raghu master to be much pleased, 1
Narad spoke again in a sweet voice:
"Ram, when once you prompted your illusory power
to delude me, Raghu king—
I had wanted to marry then, lord, 2

and why did you not let me?”
“Hear me, sage, for I tell you earnestly:
those who worship me, forsaking all other hopes,
3 I protect eternally
as a mother watches over a baby.
If a small child runs to grab at fire or a snake
his mother saves him, holding him back.
4 When that son matures, his mother
loves him still, but not so watchfully as before.
A wise one is like my grown-up son,
and my simple-hearted servant, like an infant.
5 My servant relies on my strength, the other, on his own,
yet both must face the foes of lust and anger.[100]
Discerning this, learned ones worship me
and, even gaining wisdom, do not forsake devotion.

43 Such forces as lust, anger, greed, and pride
make up the mighty army of delusion.
Yet among these, the most terrible and tormenting
is woman—illusion’s very embodiment.

1 *Purāṇs,* Vedas, and holy ones all declare, sage,
that woman is springtime for the forest of folly.[101]
For lakes of meditative prayer, austerity, and restraint,
woman is searing summer, desiccating them all.
2 For the frogs of lust, rage, pride, and jealousy,
she is the very rains at which they rejoice.
For the massed lilies of wicked wants,
she is their ever-delightful autumn season,
3 but for all the clustered lotuses of piety,

her languid pleasure is winter's killing frost;
then, the thorny weed beds of egoism
flourish at the advent of woman's early spring.
For gladdening the owl flocks of sin, 4
woman is a pitch-dark night,
and for the fish of wisdom, strength, virtue, and truth,
she is an angler's hook—so discerning ones say.

A lovely young woman is the root of vices, 44
giver of pain, and mine of all sorrows!
Knowing this in my soul,
sage, I hindered you."

When he heard the Raghu lord's pleasing speech, 1
the sage's body thrilled and his eyes grew moist.
"What other lord," he thought, "would act like this,
from pure affection and love for his servant?
Those who fail to worship such a lord, relinquishing 2
fallacy,
are paupers in wisdom and luckless dullards."
Then Sage Narad spoke with reverence,
"You are supremely insightful, Ram,
so tell me the distinguishing signs of saintly ones, 3
hero of the Raghus, who shatters rebirth's dread."
Ram said, "Indeed, sage, I will tell you the virtues
by which the holy hold me firmly in their power.
Victorious over the six sins, faultless, desireless,[102] 4
unwavering, austere, pure, and grounded in joy,
endlessly wise, without wants, eating but little,
poets, scholars, and yogis devoted to truth

5 are vigilant, respectful of others, free of pride,
steadfast, supremely skilled in the way of dharma,

45 abodes of merit, without worldly sorrow,
and freed from doubt.
Apart from my holy feet, they cherish
neither their bodies nor their homes.

1 Embarrassed to hear of their own virtues,
they greatly rejoice in hearing those of others.
Impartial and calm, never straying from prudence,
they are good natured and affectionate to all.
2 Practicing mantra repetition, austerity, restraint, and
abstinence,
they love the feet of gurus, Govinda,* and holy seers.
Showing faith, forgiveness, friendship, mercy,
and delight, they guilelessly adore my feet
3 with detachment, discernment, humility, wisdom,
and understanding in accord with Veda and *purāṇa*.
Never indulging in hypocrisy, self-pride, or arrogance,
they do not dream of setting foot on a wrong path,
4 but ever sing and hear of my playful acts,
and are unselfishly devoted to others' welfare.
Sage, the virtues of holy ones are too numerous
for even Sharada and the Veda to extoll.

5 Not even Sharada and Shesh can extoll them"—Narad
but heard this and fell prostrate, clasping those lovely feet.

* An epithet of Vishnu, commonly associated with Krishna.

Thus did the friend of the lowly, the merciful Lord,
tell of his devotees' merits with his own lips.
After bowing his head again and again
at those holy feet, Narad left for Brahma's realm.
Fortunate are they, says Tulsidas, who abandon
all other recourse to be dyed in the color of Hari.

Those people who sing or listen to 46a
the pure fame of Ravan's foe
gain unshakable devotion to Ram
without renunciation, mantra repetition, or yoga.

A young girl's body is like the flame of a lamp. 46b
Oh mind! Do not become a hapless moth,
but worship Ram, abandoning lust and pride,
and always keep the company of the holy.

[The end of the third stair of the *Rāmcaritmānas*,
which annihilates all impurities of the Kali Age.][103]

# *The Kingdom of Kishkindha*

That pair—lovely as white jasmine and blue lotus,[1] 1
supremely powerful, abodes of wisdom,
endowed with beauty, bearing mighty bows,
worshiped by the Veda, cherishing cows and seers,
assuming human form by artifice as foremost of Raghus,
shields of true dharma, benefactors of all beings,
earnestly searching for Sita, those two wayfarers—
may they grant us devotion.

Arisen from the ocean of *brahma* to become 2
the invincible annihilator of the Kali Age's filth,
and which, in the full moon of Lord Shambhu's
lovely countenance, shines in eternal splendor,
the remedy for the ills of worldly rebirth,
giver of bliss, and the very life of glorious Janaki—
the nectar of Ram's name. How blessed
are the worthy ones who eternally sip it!

Knowing it to be the birthplace of liberation, 0a
the treasury of wisdom and destroyer of sin,
where Shambhu and Bhavani* reside—
how could one not serve sacred Kashi?[2]

He who drank the dreadful poison 0b
that was scorching all the gods—
why, foolish mind, do you not worship him,
for who is as merciful as Lord Shankar?[3]

* Shiva and Parvati.

1 Then the lord of the Raghus moved on
and approached Mount Rishyamuk,
where, with his ministers, Sugriv dwelled.
Seeing those incomparably mighty heroes coming,
2 he was terrified and said, "Listen, Hanuman—
these two men embody great strength and beauty.
Taking a Brahman student's shape, go see them,
reckon in your heart, and then inform me by signs.
3 If they are sent by wicked-minded Bali,[4]
I will flee at once, abandoning this summit."
Taking a Brahman's form, the monkey went there,
bowed his head, and began to inquire:
4 "Who are you, dark- and fair-bodied men,
heroes in Kshatriya guise, roaming this wood?
Treading this rough terrain on tender feet,
why do you wander the forest, masters,
5 your delicate, beguiling, and handsome limbs
suffering its insufferable sun and wind?
Could you be among the three great gods,
or could you two be Nar and Narayan?[5]

1 Or even—creation's cause, deliverer from rebirth,
and destroyer of earth's burden—
might you be the Lord of the universe,
taken incarnation as man?"

1 "We are sons of Kosala's king, Dasarath," said Ram,
"come to the forest, obeying our father's order,
Ram and Lakshman by name, two brothers,

and a most beautiful young woman was with us.
Here in the woods, a night-stalker stole Vaidehi, 2
Brahman, and it is in search of her that we roam.
But now that I have explained our doings,
tell us, good Brahman, your own story."
Recognizing the Lord, he fell prostrate, clutching his feet, 3
and that joy of his, Uma, cannot be described.[6]
His body thrilled and he was speechless
as he beheld the Lord's most lovely guise.
Then he composed himself and uttered praise, 4
his heart rejoicing to recognize his own master.
"It was only right for me to inquire of you, lord,
but how do you question me, like an ordinary man?
Impelled by your maya, I wander, deluded, 5
and so could not recognize my lord.

I am stupid to start with, gripped by delusion, 2
perverse in heart, and ignorant,
and moreover, you—the supreme Lord
and friend of the lowly—deluded me.

Though I harbor many faults, master, 1
yet may my lord not forget his servant.
Master, the soul is deluded by your maya,
and saved solely by your loving kindness.
Moreover, I swear by you, Raghu hero, 2
that I know no worship or spiritual practice.
Servant and son, trusting in master and mother,
live unconcerned, assured of their nurture."

3 With this, he fell, all undone, at Ram's feet,
revealing his own form, his heart filled with love.
Then the Raghu lord lifted him into his embrace,
soothing him with the water of his own tears.
4 "Monkey, listen: do not think yourself worthless,
for you are twice as dear to me as Lakshman.[7]
Everyone declares me to be impartial,
yet I love my servant who relies on no other.

3 Such a dependent is one whose understanding
never wavers from this conviction, Hanuman:
'I am a servant, and my master is the supreme Lord,
embodiment of all created beings.'"

1 Seeing his lord's favor, the son of the wind*
rejoiced at heart and shed all his anguish.
"Master, the king of monkeys lives on this hill—
he is Sugriv and is your own servant.
2 Make a friendship pact with him, master,
and, knowing his wretchedness, relieve his fear.
He will order a search for Sita
and send millions of monkeys in all directions."
3 Having thus explained the whole matter,
he placed the two men on his back.[8]
When Sugriv beheld Ram
he reckoned his birth most blessed,
4 and saluted him reverently, bowing at his feet,
but the Raghu lord and his brother embraced him.

* Hanuman, son of Vayu.

Musing on this kindness, the monkey thought—
"Oh God, will they truly cherish one such as me?"

Then Hanuman recounted 4
their respective stories in full,
and making purifying fire the witness,
forged between them a bond of steadfast love.

They pledged mutual love, concealing nothing, 1
and Lakshman fully recounted Ram's deeds.
With tears in his eyes, Sugriv declared,
"Mithila's daughter* will be found, master!
For once, when I was sitting here, 2
conferring with my ministers,
I saw her going across the sky,
wailing, in the grip of a stranger.
'Ram, Ram, oh Ram!' she was crying, 3
and seeing us, she cast down a garment."[9]
At Ram's request, it was produced at once,
and he held it to his breast and greatly grieved.
Sugriv said, "Listen to me, Raghu hero— 4
give up your grief and be resolute in heart.
I offer my services in every way
so that Janaki may return to rejoin you."

Gladdened by his friend's speech, 5
the ocean of mercy and paragon of might

* Sita.

inquired of him, "But tell me, Sugriv,
the reason why you live in this wood."

1 Sugriv said, "Master, Bali and I are brothers
who were indescribably devoted to one another.
A demon named Mayavi, a son of Maya,[10]
once came to our settlement, lord.
2 In the dead of night, he bellowed at our city gate,
and Bali could never suffer a foe's challenge.
So Bali rushed out, and seeing him, the other fled,
and then I, too, set out after my brother.
3 The demon entered a mountain cavern
and then Bali instructed me,
"Keep vigil for me for a fortnight,
but if I do not return, assume I am slain."
4 I stayed there, foe of Khar, for a full month,
until a great stream of blood came forth.
I thought, "He slew Bali and will come and kill me,"
blocked the cave mouth with a boulder, and fled.
5 The ministers, seeing the city without a lord,
insisted on giving me the kingship.
But Bali slew that demon and came back,
and seeing me, his heart grew hostile.
6 He thrashed me soundly, like an enemy,
and took everything I had, even my wife.
In terror of him, merciful Raghu hero,
I roamed distraught through all the worlds.
7 Because of a curse, he cannot come here,
yet even so I live in constant dread."

Hearing his servant's grief, the benefactor of the lowly
spoke, his great arms throbbing with excitement—

"Listen to me, Sugriv: I will slay that Bali 6
with a single arrow,
and though he takes refuge with Brahma
and Rudra,* his life will not be spared!

Those who are not saddened by a friend's sorrow— 1
even to glance their way would be a great sin.
Consider the mountain of one's own cares as dust motes,
but a friend's dust-like sorrow equal to Mount Meru.
Those who do not naturally have this perspective— 2
how do such fools ever blunder into a friendship?
To guide a friend from evil paths to good,
to reveal his virtues and conceal his faults,
to freely give and take, harboring no inner doubts, 3
always assisting to the limit of one's strength
and, in time of crisis, with hundredfold affection—
such, Veda declares, are the qualities of a true friend.[11]
But one who concocts sweet words to one's face 4
and then deviously betrays one behind one's back,
whose mind is crooked as a serpent's course, brother—
such a false friend is best abandoned.
A conniving servant, stingy king, loose woman, 5
and false friend—these four are like piercing pain.
Forget your cares, friend, rely on my strength,

* A fearsome form of Shiva.

and I will fully attend to all your affairs."
6 Then Sugriv said, "But listen, Raghu hero,
Bali is immensely strong and resolute in battle,"
and he showed the bones of Dundubhi and the palm trees,
but the Raghu lord dealt with them effortlessly.[12]
7 Seeing Ram's limitless might, Sugriv's love increased
and his conviction grew that Ram would slay Bali.
Laying his head, again and again, at Ram's feet,
the monkey monarch recognized his lord and rejoiced.
8 Then, his wisdom awakened, he spoke—
"By your grace, master, my mind has been steadied.
Happiness, riches, family, and fame—
let me relinquish all these and just serve you!
9 All these are obstacles in devotion to Ram;
so say the holy ones who adore your feet.
Worldly foes and friends, joys and woes,
are maya's creations, not the ultimate goal.
10 Bali is really my great benefactor, by whose grace
you met me, Ram, and relieved my anguish.
In a dream, he with whom one fights
one recognizes on waking, much to one's chagrin.
11 But now, lord, grant me such grace that I may
leave all and just worship you day and night!"
Hearing the monkey's world-weary speech,
Ram the bow bearer merely smiled and said,
12 "All that you say is quite true,
friend, yet my word can never prove false."[13]
Said Bhushundi, "Like a street performer's monkey,
all dance at Ram's bidding, king of birds—so Veda declares."[14]

Taking Sugriv with him, the Raghu master 13
set out, bow and arrows in his hands.
Then the Raghu lord sent Sugriv ahead,
who, gaining courage, approached and roared.
As soon as he heard him, Bali rushed out, enraged, 14
but his wife clutched his feet and admonished him—
"My lord, those with whom Sugriv has allied
are two brothers, glorious and all-powerful,
sons of Kosala's king—Lakshman and Ram. 15
They can defeat Death himself in battle!"

Bali said, "Listen, my timid darling: 7
the Raghu lord is just and impartial,
and even if he were to slay me,
then I would be with my master."[15]

So saying, that most prideful one went forth, 1
considering Sugriv to be like a wisp of straw.
The two grappled and Bali much taunted him,
landing punches and bellowing loudly.
Sugriv was overwhelmed and ran away 2
from a rain of blows like thunderbolts.
"Merciful Raghu hero, it is as I said—
he is no brother of mine, but my death!"
Ram said, "You two brothers look so alike, 3
and confused by this, I did not strike him."
Then he touched Sugriv's body with his hand;
it became like adamant and free of all pain.
Ram placed a flower garland around his neck, 4
and, giving him great vigor, sent him out again.

Then all manner of fighting resumed
as the Raghu lord watched from behind a tree.

8 Yet despite all his stratagems and strength,
Sugriv grew afraid and felt vanquished.
Then at last Ram drew and fired an arrow
that struck Bali in the heart.

1 At the arrow's impact, he fell to the ground, senseless,
but then sat up, seeing the Lord before him,
his dark body crowned by matted locks,
with red-tinged eyes, holding arrows and upraised bow.
2 Gazing long, Bali focused his mind on Ram's feet;
recognizing the Lord, he reckoned his life fulfilled.
With love in his heart but harsh words on his lips,
he looked toward Ram and said,
3 "You incarnated for dharma's sake, master,
yet you struck me like a stalking hunter!
Am I your foe, and is only Sugriv dear to you?
For what fault, master, would you slay me?"
4 Ram replied, "A young brother's wife, a sister, son's wife,
and virgin maid—these four are alike, knave.
If anyone looks at them with lustful intent,
then to slay him is no sin!
5 Fool, you were so full of vainglory
that you gave no ear to your wife's admonitions
and, even knowing he was under my protection,
you wanted to kill Sugriv, arrogant wretch."

Then Bali said, "Ram, before my master 9
my wiles will not work.
But am I still a sinner, lord,
having come to you in my last moments?"

As soon as Ram heard these humble words 1
he stroked Bali's head with his hand, saying,
"I will heal your body; restrain your departing breath."
But Bali replied, "Treasury of mercy!
Sages strive in birth after birth, 2
and yet, when dying, are unable to utter 'Ram.'
He—by the power of whose name, Shiva in Kashi
gives imperishable salvation equally to all—
has himself come, in person, before my eyes. 3
Will such a chance, lord, occur again?[16]

He is visible to my eyes, whom the sacred chants 4
eternally hail as 'Not this, not that...'
and whom sages, conquering breath and mind
and restraining the senses, in meditation but rarely attain.
Knowing me to be in the grip of powerful pride, lord,
you tell me to hold onto this body of mine.
Yet what fool would hack down heaven's tree
to build a fence around a thorny acacia?[17]

Now, master, look on me with compassion 5
and grant the boon that I crave:
in whatever womb I take birth, impelled by karma,
let me adore the feet of Ram.

And this son of mine, my equal in courtesy and might—
beneficent lord, accept him
and taking his hand, lord of gods and humans,
make Angad your own servant!

10 With firmly focused love for Ram's feet,
Bali relinquished his body,
as though a great elephant, quite unaware,
let a flower garland slip from his neck.

1 Ram sent Bali to his own supreme abode
as all the townsfolk ran up, distraught.
Widow Tara made much lamentation,
her hair unbound, heedless of her body.
2 Seeing Tara's anguish, the Raghu lord
gave her wisdom that dispelled her ignorance.
"Earth, water, fire, space, and air—
fabricated of these five, the body is most base.
3 That body appears asleep before you now,
yet its soul is eternal, so for whom do you weep?"
When her wisdom awoke, she fell at his feet,
to ask and receive the boon of supreme devotion.
4 Shiva said, "Uma, like wooden marionettes,
all are made to dance by Ram, master puppeteer."
Then Ram gave Sugriv an order
and he performed the sanctioned funeral rites.
5 Ram instructed his younger brother,
"Go and bestow kingship on Sugriv."
Bowing their heads at the Raghu lord's feet
and inspired by his command, they all left.

Lakshman quickly summoned an assembly 11
of townsfolk and Brahmans,
and gave the kingship to Sugriv,
and to Angad, the post of heir apparent.

“Uma, there is no benefactor like Ram in this world— 1
not even guru, father, mother, brother, or lord.
For it is the way of all gods, humans, and sages
to bestow affection only out of self-interest.
Obsessed, day and night, by fear of Bali, 2
his body wounded, breast burning with anxiety—
that same Sugriv was made the king of monkeys,
for the Raghu hero’s nature is pure mercy.
If one knowingly abandons such a lord, 3
why wouldn’t one fall into a web of woes?”
Then Ram again summoned Sugriv
and gave much instruction in royal statecraft.
The lord said, “Listen Sugriv, monkey monarch— 4
I will enter no town for fourteen years.
The hot season is past and the rains have come,
so I will make camp on this nearby hill.
Together with Angad, rule your realm, 5
but always keep my task in your heart.”
When Sugriv went back home,
Ram made his abode on Mount Pravarshan.

The gods had already chosen a cave 12
in that mountain and made it attractive, saying,
“Ram, the treasury of grace, will come
and make his abode here for some time.”

1 The lovely wood was in flower and most glorious;
swarms of bees hummed, greedy for nectar,
and excellent tubers, roots, fruits, and leaves
appeared in abundance, once the Lord had come.
2 Beholding that charming, incomparable peak,
the sovereign of gods stayed there with his brother.
Assuming the forms of bees, birds, and beasts,
gods, perfected ones, and sages served their Lord.
3 That forest became an embodiment of auspiciousness
after Lakshmi's lord came to abide there.
Upon a lovely, luminous crystalline boulder
the two brothers would happily sit
4 as Ram told his young brother numerous tales
of devotion, detachment, statecraft, and wisdom.
It was monsoon season, and clouds covered the sky,
rumbling most pleasingly.

13 "Look, Lakshman," Ram said, "how peacocks
dance at the sight of the rainclouds,
just as dispassionate householders rejoice
when they see a true devotee of Vishnu.

1 In the heavens, clouds thunder boastfully,
and my heart, bereft of my beloved, is fearful.
Within them, lightning flashes fleetingly,
like the inconstant love of wicked ones.
2 Clouds bend close to earth, releasing rain,
as the learned are humbled on gaining wisdom,
and the hills bear the assault of their drops
as holy ones suffer the speech of sinners.

Small streams swell, crumbling their banks, 3
as the wicked, gaining a little wealth, put on airs.
Striking the ground, the water turns muddy,
like the soul enveloped by cosmic illusion.
The ponds gradually fill with water 4
as virtues accumulate in good people,
and the water of rivers, flowing into the sea,
becomes still, like a soul who has found the Lord.

The earth turns green, and so lush with grass 14
that paths can no longer be distinguished,
just as, with the spread of heretical doctrines,
true scriptures become hidden.

Everywhere, the pleasant croaking of frogs 1
is like groups of students chanting the Veda.
Countless trees send forth fresh shoots,
like discernment growing in an aspirant's heart.
Swallowwort and camel thorn lose their leafy cover,[18] 2
as the work of the wicked is undone in a righteous realm.
Dust is now nowhere to be found,
as dharma is dispelled once one yields to anger.
The fields are lovely, dense with new crop, 3
like the abundant wealth of an altruist,
but in the darkness of cloudy nights, fireflies glimmer
like assemblies of heretical hypocrites.
Field borders are breached by pounding rain, 4
as women are ruined by becoming independent,
and diligent farmers weed their lands,
as the wise root out error, arrogance, and pride.

5 Ruddy geese are nowhere to be seen,
just as dharma flees at the dark age's onset.
In flooded sand flats, even grass cannot take root,
as lust does not arise in the heart of Hari's devotee.
6 The lovely earth teems with myriad life forms,
as subjects multiply under a righteous regime.
Here and there, many tired wayfarers are stranded,
like the bodily senses when wisdom dawns.[19]

15a At times, a mighty wind blows,
dispersing clouds on every side,
just as, with the birth of one wicked son,
a family's virtues are destroyed.

15b Sometimes there is dense darkness by day,
and at times the sun breaks through,
just as knowledge is ruined or reborn
when one finds bad company or good.

1 Now the rains have ended and *śarad* has come,
that most lovely season. Look, Lakshman—
the fields are covered with plumes of reeds,[20]
as if the rains, grown old, are showing gray hair.
2 When the star Agastya rises, paths become dry,
just as contentment dries up greed.
The clear water of rivers and ponds is as lovely
as saintly hearts freed of pride and delusion,
3 and their waters gradually recede,
as the wise slowly shed selfish attachments.

Knowing it is *śarad,* the wagtail returns,[21]
like the merit, in due time, of virtuous deeds.
Free of mud and dust, earth is as glorious 4
as the statecraft of a prudent king,
but as water levels fall, fish grow anxious,
like dependent kin when family fortunes wane.[22]
The firmament, clear and cloudless, is as fair 5
as one who renounces all hopes to rely on Hari.
Here and there, light seasonal showers
are like rare ones who attain devotion to me.

Now kings, ascetics, merchants, and beggars 16
leave their cities and go forth happily,
as those in life's four stages abandon arduous effort
when they gain devotion to the Lord.[23]

Fish who dwell in deep water are contented, 1
as those taking refuge in Hari are utterly undisturbed,
and ponds, abloom with lotuses, appear as splendid
as when transcendent God becomes manifest.
Amid the distinctive drone of noisy bees 2
all kinds of birds give out lovely calls,
but when night falls, ruddy geese grow as gloomy[24]
as scoundrels eyeing others' wealth.
Pied cuckoos cry incessantly, plagued by thirst,[25] 3
like foes of Shiva, who never find happiness.
At night, the moon relieves the season's heat
as the sight of holy ones banishes sins.
Spying the moon, flocks of *cakor* birds 4

gaze enraptured, like devotees who have found Hari.
Mosquitoes and flies expire, dreading winter's chill,
as enmity to the twice-born destroys a clan.

17 Earth's teeming life forms, rain-spawned,
disappear with *śarad's* onset,
as do the hosts of doubt and fallacy
when one meets a true teacher.

1 The rains are over and clear weather is come,
but brother, we have had no news of Sita!
The moment I learn any tidings at all,
I will instantly defeat even Death to regain her.
2 Wherever she may be, if she is alive,
I will exert myself, brother, to bring her back.
But now, even Sugriv has forgotten me,
having gained kingdom, treasure, city, and wife.
3 The very arrow with which I killed Bali—
with that same one, tomorrow, I may slay this fool."
Shiva observed, "But can he, by whose grace pride
and delusion vanish, ever experience anger, Uma?
4 His acts are grasped only by enlightened sages,
committed to loving the Raghu hero's feet."[26]
When Lakshman saw the Lord enraged,
he hefted his bow and took arrows in hand.

18 But then Ram, the epitome of mercy,
instructed his younger brother—
"Dear one, merely give a good fright
to our friend Sugriv, and bring him here."

Meanwhile, the son of the wind* reflected, 1
"Sugriv has forgotten Ram's task."
He approached him, bowed at his feet,
and proffered the four kinds of counsel.[27]
When he heard, Sugriv became utterly terrified 2
and said, "Sensual desire robbed me of my wits.
But now, son of the wind, dispatch messengers
to wherever our simian bands abide,
and say that any who do not come within a fortnight 3
will be slain by my own hand."
Then Hanuman summoned the messengers,
greeting them with immense respect,
and sternly but affectionately instructed them.[28] 4
Bowing before him, they all departed.
Just then, Lakshman came to the city,
and seeing his rage, monkeys fled in all directions.

Then Lakshman raised his bow and declared, 19
"I will burn the city to ashes!"
At this, perceiving the panic in the town,
Bali's son, Angad, came forward.

With meek entreaty, he bowed low, 1
and Lakshman amicably extended his hand.[29]
When word of Lakshman's rage reached his ears,
the king of monkeys, distraught with fear, said:
"Hanuman, listen to me—take Tara with you 2
to humbly petition and conciliate the prince!"

* Hanuman.

Hanuman went there with Tara,
saluted Lakshman's feet, and extolled the Lord's fame.
3 With great deference, they brought him to the palace,
washed his feet, and seated him on a couch.
At last the monkey monarch bowed before him,
but, grasping his arms, Lakshman embraced him.
4 Sugriv said, "Master, there is no intoxication like lust,
which, in an instant, deludes even the hearts of sages."
Well pleased by his humble speech,
Lakshman gave him much counsel,
5 and the son of the wind told in detail
of the dispatching of legions of messengers.

20 Then Sugriv set out joyfully,
taking along Angad and other monkeys,
and, letting Ram's brother precede them,
came to where the Raghu lord was staying.

1 Laying his head at Ram's feet, Sugriv saluted him
and said, "Master, I am not in the least at fault,
for your divine illusion is all powerful,
Ram, and spares only one whom you favor.
2 Gods, humans, and sages are overpowered by desire, lord,
and I am but a lowly beast, a most lustful monkey.
One who is not struck by the arrow of female eyes,
who stays alert in the dark night of fierce anger,
3 who has not let his neck be bound in greed's noose—
such a one can only be like you, Raghu king!
This virtue does not accrue from spiritual practice,
and solely by your grace do rare ones attain it."

Then the Raghu lord smiled and said, 4
"You are as dear to me as Bharat, brother.
And now, set your mind to the endeavor
whereby we may gain news of Sita."

While they thus conversed intimately, 21
the monkey host arrived,
and a vast army of simians, of many colors,
was seen in all directions.

"I saw that host of warriors, Uma," said Shiva, 1
"and only a fool would want to count them.
They came and bowed their heads at Ram's feet,
and beholding his face, all recognized their master.
There was not a single monkey in that army 2
of whose well-being Ram did not inquire—
and this was nothing extraordinary for the Lord,
for the Raghu king is universal and all-pervading."[30]
With his leave, they stood around him 3
as Sugriv began to instruct them.
"For Ram's purpose and as a favor to me,
go forth, monkey hosts, in the four directions.
Go and search for Janak's daughter 4
and return within a month's span, brothers.
Anyone coming past this limit, and without news,
I will be obliged to have put to death.

As soon as they heard his order, all the monkeys 22
immediately sped forth in every direction,

and then Sugriv summoned
Angad, Nal, and Hanuman.[31]

1 "Listen to me, Nil, Angad, Hanuman,
and Jambavan, for you are steadfast and wise.
All you experienced warriors—go south together,
and inquire of everyone concerning Sita.
2 Devote mind, body, and speech to that effort
so as to fulfill Ramchandra's task.
One worships the sun with one's back; fire, face forward,[32]
but a master warrants wholehearted, sincere service.
3 Renouncing illusion, one should pursue salvation
that erases all the sorrows arising from rebirth.
And the real reward of taking on a body, brothers, is this:
to adore Ram, abandoning all desires.
4 That one alone knows virtue and alone is fortunate
who fervently loves the Raghu hero's feet."
Taking his leave, they bowed before him
and left joyfully, remembering the Raghu lord.
5 Lastly, the son of the wind bowed his head,
and the Lord, mindful of the task ahead, called him near.
Stroking Hanuman's head with his lotus-like hand
and knowing him to be his own, he gave him his ring,
6 saying, "Reassure Sita in every possible way, telling
of my might and longing for her, then quickly return."
Hanuman considered his birth's purpose fulfilled
and left, keeping the treasury of mercy in his heart.
7 For, although the Lord knows all things,
that protector of gods kept to kingly protocol.[33]

All the monkeys went forth to search 23
woods, rivers, lakes, and mountain caves,
their minds absorbed in Ram's task
and forgetful of bodily attachments.

Wherever they encountered a night-stalker, 1
they dispatched him with a rain of blows.
Thoroughly combing forests and hills,
if they met a sage, they gathered around him.[34]
Afflicted by thirst, they grew desperate, 2
lost in dense forest where they found no water.
Hanuman thought to himself,
"Without water to drink, they are losing the will to live."
He climbed a nearby summit to look on all sides, 3
and at the mouth of a cavern, beheld a wonder:
flights of water birds—geese, herons, and *haṃsas*—
were entering it in great numbers.
The son of the wind came down from the peak 4
and brought them all to see that cavern.
Placing Hanuman in the lead,
they entered the cave without delay.

Proceeding, they beheld a lovely garden grove 24
and a lake abloom with clustered lotuses,
and nearby, a splendid palace
in which sat a woman radiant with ascetic power.

From a respectful distance, they all bowed to her 1
and, at her inquiry, gave account of themselves.
Then she said to them, "You may drink this water

and partake of these many delectable fruits."
2 And so they bathed and ate sweet fruits,
and then they all once more came to her.
She recounted her whole story, and said,
"Now I will go to where the Raghu king abides.[35]
3 Close your eyes to exit this cavern and go forth,
and you will assuredly find Sita, so do not grieve."
Closing, then reopening their eyes, the heroes
all found themselves standing on the seashore.
4 Then that woman went to the Raghu master
to lay her head at his lotus-like feet.
She made many prayerful entreaties,
and the Lord gave her unshakable devotion.

25 Then she went to the forest of Badri[36]
in obedience to the Lord's command,
cherishing in her heart Ram's feet,
which unborn Brahma and great Shiva worship.

1 Meanwhile, the monkeys were pondering,
for the allotted time had passed, their task unfulfilled.
Conferring, they all said to one another,
"With no news to bring, what will we do, brothers?"
2 Angad declared with tearful eyes,
"One way or the other, we are doomed.
We have found no news of Sita here,
and if we go back there, the monkey lord will kill us.
3 After my father was slain, he would have killed me, too,
but for Ram's protection—it was no kindness on his part!"
Again and again, Angad told them all,

"No doubt about it: we are as good as dead."
Those simian heroes heard Angad's words 4
and could not speak, but wept profusely.
For a moment they remained sunk in thought,
and then they all began to speak:
"Without having gotten news of Sita, 5
we shall not go back, prudent prince!"
With this, they went to the salty sea's edge,
spread *darbha* grass, and stoically sat down.[37]
Jambavan,* perceiving Angad's dismay, 6
gave edifying and pertinent counsel—
"Son, do not take Ram to be a mere man.
Know him as formless *brahma*—unconquerable, unborn—
and we, his servants, are supremely fortunate 7
to steadfastly love God made manifest.

Whenever, of his own free will, the Lord comes down 26
for the sake of gods, earth, cows, and the twice-born,
worshipers of manifest God keep his company,
forsaking all forms of spiritual liberation."

While many discourses of this sort were spoken, 1
in a mountain cave, vulture Sampati was listening.
Coming out and seeing many monkeys, he said,
"The Lord of the world has given me a meal.[38]
Today I will devour all of these, 2
for I have long been dying of hunger,
never getting enough food to fill my belly.

* The aged and wise king of bears.

But today, all at once, fate has provided it!"
3 Frightened by hearing the vulture's words,
the monkeys said, "Now we know our death is certain!"
They all arose to look at the scavenger bird,
and Jambavan was especially disheartened.
4 Then Angad thought to himself and spoke up—
"None was more blessed than the vulture Jatayu,
for he gave up his body in Ram's cause
and, supremely fortunate, went to Hari's realm."
5 Hearing words imbued, for him, with joy and sorrow,
the great bird approached, alarming the monkeys.
But he reassured them and asked for details,
so they told him Jatayu's whole story,
6 and when Sampati heard of his brother's deeds,
he extolled the greatness of the Raghu lord.

27 Then he said, "Carry me to the ocean's edge,
so that I may make his funerary offering.[39]
Then I will give you helpful guidance,
and you will find her whom you seek."

1 After performing his younger brother's rites at the shore,
he told them his story: "Listen, brave monkeys—
in the first flush of youth, we two brothers
flew high into the heavens, close to the sun.
2 Jatayu could not bear the heat and turned back,
but I, in my pride, flew even closer to the god.
From his boundless energy, my wings caught fire
and I fell to earth, shrieking in agony.

There was a sage named Chandrama* 3
who took pity at the sight of me.
He taught me much wisdom
and liberated me from bodily pride.
'In the Treta Age,' he said, '*brahma* will take human form 4
and his wife will be stolen by the king of demons.
The Lord will dispatch messengers to seek her;
when you meet them, you will be purified
and your wings will regrow, so do not worry. 5
Show them the whereabouts of Sita.'
The sage's prophecy has come true today,
and now, hearing my words, complete the Lord's task.
Atop Mount Trikuta stands the city of Lanka; 6
there Ravan resides, secure and fearless,
and therein is a grove of *aśoka* trees,
where Sita sits, forever plunged in grief.

I see her, though you cannot, 28
for we vultures have far-ranging sight.
Alas that I have grown so old, or else
I would surely do something to help you.

Only one who can leap a hundred leagues of ocean[40] 1
and is keenly intelligent can execute Ram's task.
But look at me and take courage in your hearts—
see how, by Ram's grace, my body is changed!
When even a sinner, recalling his name, 2
crosses over the boundless sea of rebirth,

* Appropriately, "Moon."

what of you, his own emissaries? Shun timidity,
and keeping Ram in your hearts, devise a plan."
3 Garuda, when the vulture had said this and departed,[41]
the monkeys' minds were wonderstruck.
Each began to extoll his own strength,
yet harbored doubt about crossing the sea.
4 "I have become aged now," said the bear king,
"and my body retains no trace of its former might.
When Khar's foe* became the triple-striding dwarf,
I was young and possessed immense strength.

29 When he suppressed Bali, the Lord's body
grew into a form beyond description.[42]
Yet I raced and, in less than an hour,
reverently circled him seven times!"

1 Angad said, "I could surely make it across,
but I feel some doubt about the return journey."
"You are entirely capable," rejoined Jambavan,
"but how can we send our mission's leader?"
2 Then the bear king said, "Hear me, Hanuman:
why do you remain silent, mighty one?
You are son of the wind, with power like his own,
a treasury of intelligence, discernment, and wisdom.
3 What task in this world is so difficult,
son, that it cannot be accomplished by you?
Your very incarnation is for Ram's work."[43]

* Ram, but here, Vishnu.

Hearing this, Hanuman grew to mountainous form,
his body golden-colored and aglow with energy, 4
like another Sumeru, king of summits.
Roaring again and again like a lion, he said,
"In merest sport, I can leap this salty sea,
slaughter Ravan along with his minions, 5
and uproot Trikuta peak and bring it here!
But I ask you, Jambavan—
instruct me in my proper task."
The bear said, "Go, son, but only do this much: 6
see Sita, and return to report news of her.
Then lotus-eyed Ram, by his own arms' might,
and taking along a monkey army just for sport—

accompanied by an army of monkeys,[44] 7
Ram will slay the night-stalkers and bring Sita back.
Then his fame, which purifies the three worlds,
will be extolled by gods, and by Narad and other sages.
One who listens to, sings, recounts, and understands it
attains the ultimate state—
and it is sung by that bee on the lotus
of the Raghu hero's feet, the servant Tulsi.

The Raghu master's fame is the cure 30a
for worldly ills, and men and women who listen to it
have all their wishes fulfilled
by Ram, the triple-headed demon's foe.*

* Trishira, a demon slain in sub-book three.

30b He whose body is dark as a blue lotus
and who is more lovely than a billion love gods—
listen to the litany of his merits—
whose name is a fowler for the birds of sin.

[The end of the fourth stair of the *Rāmcaritmānas,*
which annihilates all impurities of the Kali Age.]

# *The Beautiful Quest*

To that supremely tranquil one—eternal, autonomous, 1
sinless,[1]
giver of the ultimate peace of liberation,
ever worshiped by Brahma, Shiva, and the serpent king,
knowable through *vedānta,* the all-pervading[2]
lord of the universe and master of the gods, named "Ram,"
Lord Hari in the artifice of a human body,
treasury of compassion, foremost of Raghus,
and crown jewel of earth's monarchs—I reverently bow.

Raghu lord, I declare in truth—and you are the omniscient 2
inner self of all beings—there is no longing in my heart but
this:
bestow on me, mightiest of Raghus, boundless devotion,
and purge my mind of lust and other failings.[3]

To him—who is the abode of matchless strength, 3
with a body like a gleaming mountain of gold,
who is wildfire in the forest of demons,
and foremost among the wise,
treasury of all virtues,
master of monkeys,
chosen emissary of the Raghu lord,
and offspring of the mighty wind—I bow in homage.[4]

To hear Jambavan's eloquent words[5] 1
brought the greatest delight to Hanuman's heart.
He said, "Wait and watch for me, brothers,
bearing your grief and living on forest fare,

2 until I return, having seen Sita—
the mission will succeed, for I feel intense joy!"
So saying, he bowed his head to them all
and happily set out, keeping the Raghu master in his heart.
3 A splendid mountain stood at the ocean's edge;
effortlessly, he sprang to its summit.
Again and again invoking the Raghu hero,
the wind's immensely mighty son leaped forth,
4 and that peak, pressed down by Hanuman's feet,
immediately sank into the netherworld.
Unerring as the Raghu lord's own arrow
was the flight of Hanuman.
5 Recognizing the Raghu lord's emissary, the ocean
told Mount Mainak, "Go and allay his fatigue."[6]

1 But Hanuman merely touched him with his hand
and then saluted him, saying,
"Until I accomplish Ram's task,
how can I take rest?"

1 The gods watched the son of the wind's progress,
and sought to gauge his singular strength and intelligence
by dispatching the mother of serpents, Surasa by name,
who approached him and hissed,
2 "Today the celestials have sent me a meal!"
To her words, the wind's son at once replied,
"When I complete Ram's errand and return
to convey news of Sita to the Lord,
3 then I will come back and enter your mouth—
I speak the truth, mother; now let me go on."

When, despite every effort, she would not yield,
Hanuman cried, "Then why don't you eat me?"
So she spread her jaws a full league wide, 4
but the monkey made his body twice that size.
The monster's maw became sixteen leagues,
and, at once, the wind's son swelled to thirty-two!
However much Surasa blew up her face 5
the monkey showed a form double to that,
but when she stretched her mouth to a hundred leagues,
the son of the wind shrank to tiny size,
shot into her jaws, then out again, 6
and, bowing his head, asked leave to depart.
She said, "That for which the gods sent me—
to plumb your wit and power—I have done.

You are indeed a treasury of both, 2
and sure to complete all of Ram's tasks."
Surasa swam off spouting blessings
and Hanuman went happily on.

Now a certain she-demon dwelt in the sea, 1
and caught flying birds by a strange magic:
when living creatures flew across the sky,
she spied their shadows on the water
and seized these, so they could not fly; 2
so she regularly ate her fill of flyers.
She tried this trick on Hanuman, too,
but the monkey divined her ruse at once.
Slaying her, the heroic son of the storm[7] 3
resolutely advanced to reach the far shore,

where he beheld the beauty of woods
abuzz with bees eager for flower nectar,
4 with all sorts of lovely trees in bloom and fruit,
and myriad birds and beasts to delight the heart.
Sighting a lofty mountain just ahead
he raced fearlessly to its summit. (Shiva said,
5 "None of this was due to the monkey's greatness, Uma,
but to the glory of that Lord who devours even Death.")
Summiting that peak, he gazed on Lanka,
an extraordinary fortress that defies description,
6 with towering ramparts surrounded by ocean
and golden battlements of dazzling brilliance—

7 a golden fortress set with sparkling gems
and crowded with splendid mansions,
a glorious city of squares and markets,
avenues and lanes, ingeniously laid out,
with hordes of elephants, horses, donkeys,
chariots, and countless throngs on foot,
and masses of night-stalkers of every size and shape,
a mighty army beyond accounting.

8 There were lovely woods, orchards, gardens, and groves,
reservoirs, pools, and cool stepwells,
and young women—human, serpentine, celestial—
with beauty to enchant the hearts of sages.
Here and there, powerful wrestlers with bodies
like great mountains roared mightily
and grappled skillfully in countless arenas
that rang with their mutual challenges.

Millions upon millions of awful-bodied warriors 9
watchfully guarded that city on all four sides,
while everywhere buffaloes, men, cattle, asses, and goats
were devoured by its wicked, night-ranging folk.
But here is the reason why Tulsidas
has lingered, just a little, to tell of them:
they will surely shed their bodies at the shrine
of the Raghu hero's arrows, and be saved.[8]

Seeing the city's myriad guards, 3
the monkey considered carefully:
"Let me take a tiny form
and enter the town by night."

He assumed gnat-like size and went to Lanka, 1
meditating on the Lord who became man-lion,[9]
but a female night-stalker, Lankini by name,[10]
challenged him: "You dare trespass, insulting me?
Don't you know my secret, fool— 2
that I feast on any would-be burglars?"
The great monkey hit her with a single punch
that sent her sprawling and spitting blood.
Then that woman—Lanka herself—recovering a little 3
and rising, joined her palms and addressed him in awe:
"Back when Brahma gave the boon to Ravan,[11]
the creator, as he departed, told me of a portent—
'When a monkey's blow renders you senseless, 4
know it will signal the night-stalkers' doom.'
Now, son, by my great good fortune
I see with my own eyes the emissary of Ram!

4 Son, even the joys of heaven and final release,
if set on one pan of a balance-scale,
together would not weigh as much as the bliss
of a moment's communion with a holy one.

1 Enter the city and accomplish all your tasks,
holding in your heart Kosala kingdom's king!"*
"Truly, poison turns to nectar, foes offer friendship,"
the crow said, "the sea shrinks to a puddle, fire turns cool,
2 and Mount Sumeru becomes a mere dust mote, Garuda,
for one on whom Ram but glances with favor."[12]
Now Hanuman took on a most tiny form,
and went into the city, remembering the Lord.
3 He searched diligently in house after house,
seeing countless formidable warriors everywhere,
and entered the ten-faced ruler's palace—
a realm of utterly unspeakable wonders.
4 The monkey beheld him sleeping there,
but saw no trace, in that abode, of Videha's daughter.†
Then he sighted one lovely mansion,
with its own Vishnu temple, set apart.[13]

5 Inscribed with Ram's weapon symbols,
that house was indescribably beautiful,
and seeing its garden of young tulsi bushes,
the noble monkey rejoiced.

* Ram.
† Sita.

"Lanka is home to myriad night-stalkers— 1
so how can any good soul reside here?"
The monkey began to inwardly ponder this,
but just then Vibhishan awoke
and began devoutly chanting, "Ram, Ram." 2
As joy of recognition filled the monkey's heart,
he thought, "I shall assuredly introduce myself to him,
for a holy one will not harm my mission."
Taking a Brahman's shape, he announced himself, 3
and Vibhishan arose and hastened there,
saluted him, inquired of his welfare, and said:
"Seer, kindly instruct me concerning yourself.
Are you, perchance, one of Hari's servants— 4
for my heart is feeling intense affection—
or even Ram himself, who so loves the wretched
that he has come to make me supremely fortunate?"

Then Hanuman told him everything: 6
Ram's story and his own name.
At the telling, their bodies thrilled with joy
and their minds were lost in recalling the Lord's virtues.

"Now hear, son of the wind, how I survive here— 1
like a hapless tongue amid clashing teeth!
Brother, knowing me to be so alone,
might the lord of the solar line ever show mercy?
My demonic form is unfit for any spiritual practice, 2
my heart holds no love for his pure feet.
Yet now I harbor hope, Hanuman,

for without the Lord's grace, no one meets a saintly one.
3 Only because the Raghu hero bestowed his favor
have you shown yourself to me."
Hanuman replied, "Listen, Vibhishan: our lord's custom
is to always lavish love on his servant.
4 Tell me, from what exalted lineage do I hail—
a restless monkey, deficient in every way?
Why, one who invokes our name at dawn
will not get anything to eat that day![14]

7 Such is my lowly state, friend, but listen—
even to me, that hero of the Raghus
has shown grace." Recalling his goodness,
tears welled up in Hanuman's eyes.

1 "Those who knowingly forget such a master
and turn away—how can they not suffer?"
And so, recounting Ram's many mercies,
they savored indescribable contentment.
2 Then Vibhishan narrated the full account
of how Janak's daughter sojourned there,
and Hanuman said, "Listen, brother,
now I wish to see Janaki, our mother."
3 Vibhishan fully disclosed the means to this,
and the wind's son bade him farewell and left.
Resuming his tiny shape, he then sped there,
to the Ashoka Grove, where Sita was staying.[15]
4 He saw her and saluted her inwardly
as she sat through the watches of the night,

her body wasted, her matted hair in one braid,
repeating Ram's virtues within her heart.

Her eyes were fixed on her own feet, 8
her mind merged in the pure feet of Ram.
The son of the wind was overcome by grief
on seeing the plight of Janak's daughter.

Staying hidden among the leaf buds, 1
he pondered, "Brother, what should I do?"
Just then, Ravan came there
with a host of women, lavishly adorned.
The scoundrel used every stratagem on Sita— 2
sweet talk, bribes, threats, and insinuation.[16]
"Hear me well, my lovely, discerning one:
Mandodari and all these other queens
I will make your handmaids, I swear it, 3
if you will even once look my way."
Setting a blade of grass between them, Vaidehi
recalled her beloved, Avadh's lord, and replied:
"Listen, Ten-head, can a firefly's flicker 4
ever prod a lotus to bloom?
Consider yourself like that, villain," said Janaki.
"Knowing nothing of the Raghu hero's arrows,[17]
you stole me on the sly, base scum— 5
don't you have even an ounce of shame?"

He heard himself likened to an insect 9
and Ram to the sun!

Listening to her stinging insults,
he drew his sword and bellowed in terrible rage:

1 “You have dared insult me, Sita, but now
I will claim your head with my keen blade!
So heed my words this instant,
pretty one, or else your life is forfeit.”
2 She replied, “Lovely as a chain of blue lotuses,
strong as an elephant’s trunk, Ten-neck, is my lord’s arm,
which alone will touch this neck, or else your cruel blade.
Hear this, villain, for it is my firm vow!
3 Oh moon-like Chandrahas, cool my fever[18]
born of the fire of longing for the Raghu lord.
Your gleaming blade flows cool and keen,”[19]
Sita said, “so lift my burden of sorrows.”
4 When he heard this, he rushed to kill her,
but Maya’s daughter, Mandodari,* dissuaded him.
So he summoned all the demon women, saying,
“Go and do your utmost to frighten Sita.
5 If, in a month, she does not obey my order,
I will draw this sword and slay her.”

10 With this, the ten-headed one went home,
leaving behind a bevy of she-demons,
trying to terrify Sita
by assuming many loathsome forms.

---

* Ravan’s chief queen.

But one among them, Trijata by name, 1
adored Ram's feet and had acquired discernment.
She called them all and related a dream, saying,
"Serve Sita now for your own good.
In my dream, a monkey set fire to Lanka 2
and slaughtered the whole demon army.
Ten-headed Ravan was mounted on an ass, naked,
with shaven pates, all twenty arms broken,
and in that state, he departed for the south,* 3
and it seemed Vibhishan took over Lanka.
The Raghu hero's victory was proclaimed in the city,
and then that lord sent for his Sita.
This dream, I solemnly avow, 4
will come true before many days."[20]
At her words, they all took fright
and fell at the feet of Janak's daughter.

Then they all scattered here and there, 11
and Sita was left to brood:
"When a month has passed,
the vile night-stalker will slay me."

With palms joined, she implored Trijata, 1
"Mother, you are my sole friend in adversity,
so find a way for me to quickly quit this body,
for separation's agony is past enduring.
Bring wood and build me a pyre, 2

* The direction of Yama, god of death.

mother, and then set it alight
to prove the truth of my love, wise woman—
for who can bear to hear that scoundrel's piercing words?"
3 At this, Trijata touched Sita's feet and admonished her,
reminding her of her lord's majesty, might, and fame.
"And it is night, dear princess; fire is unavailable"—
so she said, and left for her own abode.
4 Sita said to herself, "Fate has turned against me—
no fire to be had, no respite from this agony!
The very sky seems dotted with embers,
yet not one blazing star will fall to earth.
5 The moon is white-hot but will not rain fire,
as if even he knows my case is hopeless.
*Aśoka* tree, listen to my entreaty:
live up to your name and lift my sorrow.
6 Your ruddy buds resemble flames,
so give me fire, for my disease is terminal."[21]
Seeing Sita's agony of separation from Ram,
that moment to the monkey seemed an aeon.

12 So Hanuman pondered in his heart,
and then cast down the ring,
as though the *aśoka* had yielded a spark.
Rejoicing, she arose and seized it.

1 Then she beheld that captivating ring,
artfully inscribed with Ram's own name.
Recognizing it, she gazed in wonder,
her heart torn between joy and grief, thinking,

"None can defeat my unvanquished Raghu lord, 2
and no conjuring can craft such a wonder."
As Sita pondered all possibilities,
Hanuman began to speak sweet words,
recounting the virtues of Ramchandra— 3
just hearing him, Sita's sorrow fled,
and she began to listen with all her heart
as he recounted the whole tale from the beginning.
Then she said, "You who tell this nectar-like story— 4
why do you not reveal yourself, brother?"
Then Hanuman approached her;
startled, she turned away and sat down.[22]
"Mother Janaki, I am Ram's emissary 5
in truth—I swear by that treasury of mercy!
I have brought this ring, mother,
given by Ram as a sign to you."
"But how," she asked, "can men join with monkeys?" 6
So he recounted the tale of their alliance.

Hearing the monkey's loving speech,[23] 13
conviction arose in Sita's heart,
and she knew him to be, in thought, deed, and word,
the servant of the sea of mercy.

Knowing him as the Lord's, her love deepened; 1
her eyes filled with tears as her body thrilled with joy.[24]
"I was drowning in the sea of separation, Hanuman,
but, dear child, you have become my boat.
Now, I entreat you, tell me of the welfare 2

of the abode of joy, Khar's foe,* and his young brother.
The Raghu prince is kind and merciful,
monkey, so why has he assumed cold indifference?
3 His natural tendency is to please his servants,
but does that Raghu lord ever remember me?
And will my eyes ever be cooled, my child,
by the sight of his lovely, cloud-dark body?"
4 Her words broke off as her eyes filled with tears.
Then she cried, "Alas, lord! I am utterly forgotten!"
Seeing Sita so anguished by separation,
the monkey spoke gentle and soothing words:
5 "Mother, the lord and Lakshman are both well,
but that most merciful one sorrows in your sorrow.
Do not feel yourself worthless, mother—
Ram's love for you exceeds even yours for him.[25]

14 Now here is the Raghu lord's message,
mother—compose yourself and listen to it."
As he said this, the monkey's voice broke
and his eyes filled with tears.

1 "Ram says, 'Separated from you, Sita,
all pleasing things have turned against me.
Budding tree-shoots sear me like embers,
night is an apocalypse, the moon, sun-hot;
2 massed lotus buds poke me like spears,
while rainclouds seem to release boiling oil.
Once-beneficent things now cause only pain—

* Ram.

cool, fragrant breezes burn like serpent's breath.
Speaking of one's sorrow lessens it somewhat, 3
but whom can I tell? No one comprehends it.
The secret of our mutual love,
dearest, my heart alone knows,
and it remains forever with you. 4
Know this to be the essence of my love.'"
Hearing her lord's message, Vaidehi
was drowned in love and lost bodily awareness.
The monkey said, "Take courage, mother. 5
Remember Ram, who delights his servants,
and drawing the Raghu lord's power into your heart,
heed my message and cast out cowardice.

The night-stalker legions are like moths, 15
the Raghu prince's arrows a mighty flame.
Take courage in your heart, mother,
and know the demons to be as good as burned!

Had the Raghu hero but received word of you, 1
that regal lord would have brooked no delay,
and when the sun of Ram's arrow rises, Janaki,
what will be left of the demon army's darkness?
I would carry you back right now, mother— 2
I swear on Ram—but I lack the lord's permission.
Bear up, mother, for a few days more,
and the Raghu hero will come with his monkeys.
He will slay the night-stalkers and take you away, 3
and divine sages will sing his fame in all the worlds!"
Sita asked, "Son, are all the monkeys small, like you?

These demons are most mighty warriors,
4 and so my heart harbors a great doubt."
At this, the monkey manifested his true form,
with a body like an immense mountain of gold—
a terror in battle, and a hero supreme.
5 Then Sita believed, and the wind god's son
shrank again to tiny form, and said:

16 "Mother, we monkeys are but branch-beasts[26]
with no great strength or wisdom,
yet by our Lord's might, even the tiniest garden snake
can gobble up Garuda, emperor of eagles."

1 Her heart was soothed by the monkey's words,
imbued with devotion, majesty, and fierce power.
Knowing him to be dear to Ram, she blessed him:
"My child, be forever an abode of strength and virtue,
2 ageless and deathless, a treasury of merit, son,
and may the Raghu lord shower his grace on you."
His ears just heard "may the Lord be gracious to you"
and Hanuman became utterly lost in love.
3 Bowing again and again at her feet,
the monkey, palms reverently joined, proclaimed:
"My aim is achieved now, mother,
by your blessing, famed as infallible.
4 But mother, I am feeling terribly hungry
just looking at all those lush fruit trees."
Sita said, "Son, this grove is guarded
by the mightiest night-stalker warriors."

He replied, “I have no fear of them, mother, 5
if you are pleased with me.”

Perceiving that the monkey was adroit 17
in both wit and warfare, Janaki said, “Go,
keeping the Raghu lord’s feet in your heart,
child, and savor those sweet fruits.”

He bowed to her and entered the garden, 1
ate fruits, and began breaking tree limbs.
Of the many warriors keeping guard there,
some he slew, and some went crying to Ravan:
“Master, a huge monkey has come 2
and is ravishing the Ashoka Garden,
devouring fruits, uprooting trees,
and crushing our sentries to pulp!”
At this, Ravan dispatched many stalwarts, 3
whom Hanuman met with a mighty roar.
He massacred all those night-stalkers, save a few,
half dead, who went back wailing.
Then Ravan sent his young son Akshay, 4
who left with a vast force of tested warriors.
At their approach, Hanuman defiantly seized a tree
and, bellowing, struck the prince a fatal blow.

Some demons he slew outright, some he crushed, 18
and some he seized and ground into the dust.
A few managed to escape, crying,
“Master, that monkey’s strength is incredible!”

1 News of his boy's death enraged Lanka's king,
who now sent his eldest, the mighty Meghnad.
"Don't slay him, son. Bind and bring him here,
so we may find out whence this monkey comes."
2 That matchless champion, vanquisher of Indra, set out,
fuming to hear of his brother's downfall.
Marking the approach of a formidable warrior,
the monkey bared his teeth and came on roaring.[27]
3 He uprooted a single immense tree
and shattered the Lankan prince's chariot,
then seized the stalwarts accompanying him
and crushed them against his sides.
4 With them dead, he turned on the prince
and they raged like two rogue elephant bulls.
Landing one square blow, Hanuman climbed a tree
while his foe momentarily fainted.
5 When he again rose, Meghnad took recourse to sorcery,
yet even this could not defeat the son of the wind.

19 So he readied the supreme weapon of Brahma,
while the monkey reflected,
"If I do not yield to the creator's own arrow,
its immense fame will be erased."

1 Meghnad fired Brahma's weapon at Hanuman,
who, even as he fell, pulverized his army.
Seeing the monkey unconscious, the demon
bound him in a serpent snare for transport.[28]
2 "But Bhavani," Shiva said, "he whose name is chanted
by wise ones to sever rebirth's bonds—

could his own messenger ever be ensnared?
The monkey got himself bound for the Lord's work!"
Hearing of his capture, night-stalkers streamed 3
into the royal assembly hall to see the wonder.
Now Hanuman beheld ten-headed Ravan's court,
of a grandeur wholly beyond expression,
where gods and world-guardians, palms joined, 4
all anxiously marked the play of Ravan's brows.
Yet even seeing this splendor, the monkey was as resolute
and fearless as Garuda entering a nest of serpents.

Observing the monkey, Ravan's ten faces 20
howled with glee and hurled insults.
But then he recalled his son's slaying,
and grief arose in his heart.

Lanka's lord spoke: "Who are you, monkey, 1
and by whose might did you ravage my grove?
Can it be that your ears have never heard of me,
scoundrel, that I see you looking so cocky?
For what offense did you kill my night-stalkers? 2
Answer, villain, or don't you value your life's breath?"
Hanuman replied, "Hear now, Ravan, of him
by whose might maya molds countless universes;
by whose power Brahma, Hari, and Shiva 3
birth, nurture, and annihilate them, Ten-head;
and the thousand-hooded serpent bears on his brow
the whole cosmos, with its mountains and woods;[29]
who assumes countless forms to protect the gods 4

and teach a lesson to scoundrels like you;
who shattered Shiva's awesome bow
and with it, the arrogance of the assembled kings;
5 who slew Khar, Dushan, Trishira, and Bali, too—[30]
all incomparably mighty warriors;

21 of him, by the merest micron of whose power
you conquered all created beings,
I am the emissary—of him,
whose own dear wife you stole![31]

1 And yes, I know all about your eminence—
how you took on thousand-armed Sahasbahu,
and battled Bali too—what glory you won!"
At these monkey jabs the demon laughed evasively.[32]
2 "I ate Your Lordship's fruit because I was hungry,
and being a monkey, broke some tree limbs.
And who doesn't cherish his own body, sir?[33]
So when your wicked guards assaulted me,
3 I struck back at them in turn,
at which point your son managed to secure me.
But I am not a bit ashamed to be bound,
for I want only to complete my lord's task.
4 Ravan, I petition you in all humility—
forsake your pride and heed my guidance.
Reflect on your own noble lineage,
shed delusion, and adore him who frees devotees of fear.
5 Of him—dread of whom terrifies even Death,
devourer of gods, demons, and all beings—

never incur the enmity!
Heed my words and give up Janaki.

The Raghu master cherishes suppliants; 22
Khar's foe is a sea of sympathy.
Seek the Lord's shelter and he will accept you,
forgetting your offense.

Set his lotus-like feet in your heart 1
and you will reign secure over Lanka.
The renown of the seer Pulastya, your grandsire,
is a spotless moon; do not become a stain on it!
Without Ram's name, speech lacks splendor— 2
observe this, abandoning arrogance and delusion—
as a naked woman lacks appeal, enemy of gods,
though comely, and all done up in ornaments.[34]
Enmity to Ram yields treasure and majesty 3
that quickly vanishes, loss even in gain,
as rivers that lack a constant source
soon revert to dry flats after the rains.
Listen to me, Ten-neck: I solemnly swear 4
that a foe of Ram has no protector.
Even a thousand Shivas, Vishnus, and Brahmas
cannot save one who is hostile to Lord Ram.

Give up egoism, delusion's dark root 23
that produces a profusion of pain,
and worship Ram, the Raghu king
and supreme God of oceanic compassion."

1 Though the monkey gave most beneficial advice,
full of devotion, discernment, dispassion, and diplomacy,
that emperor of arrogance only guffawed and said,
"It seems I landed a smart monkey-guru!
2 Villain, your death is imminent,
yet, wretch, you would start lecturing me!"
"Just the opposite will occur," Hanuman replied,
"for I clearly perceive your befuddled mind."
3 Hearing this, Ravan flew into a rage, and roared,
"Won't someone snuff out this fool's life, and fast?"
At this, night-stalkers came running to kill him,
but Vibhishan approached with wise ministers.
4 Bowing his head, he very humbly submitted,
"To slay an emissary would violate statecraft,
master, so ordain some other punishment."
All affirmed the soundness of this advice.
5 Ten-neck heard them and snorted,
"Then just rough up the monkey and pack him off.

24 But wait—the tail is a monkey's pride and joy,
so heed my instruction, all of you:
wrap his up in oil-soaked rags
and then set it on fire!

1 The monkey will go back there tail-less,
then the fool will bring that master of his,
whose praises he so fulsomely sings,
so I can have a look at his might."
2 When he heard this, Hanuman smiled to himself:

"I believe that Sharada has come to my aid!"[35]
But the dense-minded demons heard Ravan's decree
and those fools went straight to their task.
Soon no cloth, oil, or ghee was left in Lanka, 3
for the monkey playfully expanded his tail.
All the demon denizens came out for the show,
to deliver a kick or heap on mockery.
To the beat of drums and loud clapping, 4
they marched him about town, then set his tail alight.
But when Hanuman saw the fire catching,
he instantly shrank to a most tiny form,
slipped his bonds, and sprang onto a gilded gable, 5
causing terror to the demon women.

At that instant, inspired by Lord Hari, 25
all forty-nine winds arose together,[36]
as, roaring with laughter,
the monkey grew till he touched the sky.

Gargantuan, yet supremely light and nimble, 1
he leaped from housetop to housetop,
till the city was ablaze and its folk crazed
by myriad ferocious, flapping flames.
They were all heard crying out, "Father, Mother! 2
Alas, who will save us now?
Didn't we warn that this is no monkey,
but some god who has taken simian guise?
Our affront to a holy one bears fruit now 3
and our city burns, as if it had no protector."

Indeed, Hanuman torched it all in an instant,
sparing only Vibhishan's dwelling.
4 Shiva said, "But the messenger of him who created
fire itself, Girija,* could therefore not be singed."
Hanuman wreaked fiery havoc in the whole of Lanka
and then bounded into the sea.

26 He extinguished his tail and refreshed himself,
then assumed tiny form once more
and stood before King Janak's daughter
in reverent attitude.

1 "Mother, please give me some token
such as the Raghu master sent with me."
So Sita removed and gave him her crest jewel[37]
and the son of the wind joyously received it.
2 "My son, convey my salutation thus:
'Though you are wholly self-sufficient, Lord,
maintain your fame as merciful to the wretched,
and lift, master, my heavy burden of affliction.'
3 Child, tell him the tale of Indra's son,
and remind the Lord of his arrow's fury.[38]
If my husband does not come within a month,
then he will not find me alive.
4 But tell me, monkey, how may I cling to life,
now that you too, son, speak of leaving me?
My heart has been cooled by your sight,
but now I face again the same awful days and nights!"

* Parvati.

Hanuman comforted and encouraged 27
Janak's daughter in diverse ways.
Then he bowed before her holy feet
and set forth to return to Ram.

As he left, he let out a thunderous roar 1
that made pregnant she-demons miscarry.
Leaping the sea, he reached the other shore
and gave a joyful shriek to his monkey cohorts.[39]
When they saw Hanuman they all exulted, 2
and then the monkeys felt as though reborn,
for his happy face and radiant form
bespoke accomplishment of Ramchandra's task.
They all embraced him and became as joyful 3
as beached and dying fish regaining water,
and headed happily back to the Raghu lord,
chattering to each other about their new adventures.
They entered the royal Madhuban Grove 4
and, with Angad's leave, ate its honey and fruit.[40]
When the guards there tried to prevent this,
they were chased away with a rain of fists.

They all ran shouting to the king: 28
"The crown prince is looting your grove!"
Sugriv heard this and rejoiced, knowing
the returned monkeys had done the Lord's task.

"If they had not gained news of Sita, 1
would they dare eat my Madhuban's fruit?"
So that monkey raja reasoned to himself,

and soon the whole party approached.
2 All bowed their heads at the feet
of their monarch, who greeted them most lovingly,
asking of their welfare. "We are well, seeing your feet,
and by Ram's grace, the task is more than done.[41]
3 Hanuman completed the mission, master,
and saved all the monkeys' lives."[42]
At this, Sugriv embraced him again,
and went with them all to the Raghu lord.
4 When Ram saw the monkeys approaching,
their task accomplished, his heart greatly rejoiced.
The two brothers were seated on a crystalline boulder,
and all the monkeys fell at their feet.

29 The Raghu lord, treasury of compassion,
embraced them with affection
and inquired of their welfare. "We fare well, master,
now that we again behold your holy feet."

1 Jambavan spoke for all: "Raghu king,
that one on whom you bestow your grace
is eternally blessed and forever well,
favored by gods, humans, and sages,
2 victorious yet humble, a sea of virtues,
whose fame shines through the three worlds.
By your mercy, lord, the whole task was completed
and today our lives are made fruitful,
3 for, master, what the wind's son accomplished,
not even a thousand tongues could tell!"
Then the glorious deeds of that son of the storm

were recounted to the Raghu lord by Jambavan.
Listening, the merciful one was greatly pleased 4
and joyfully clasped Hanuman to his breast.
"Tell me, friend, how Janak's daughter
abides there, and how she yet clings to life."

Hanuman said, "Your name is her sentry, day and night, 30
her remembrance of you is a gate, sealed tight.
Her gaze stays locked on her own feet—
so by what street could life's breath flee?

But when I left, she gave me her crest jewel"— 1
taking it, the Raghu lord pressed it to his heart—
"and then, master, with tear-filled eyes
King Janak's daughter uttered these few words:
'Touch the feet of my lord and his brother, and say, 2
"You are friend to the poor and succor of the wretched,
and I adore your feet in thought, deed, and word—
so for what sin, master, have I been forsaken?
There is one fault, yes, to which I admit— 3
that, parted from you, my life's breath did not depart.
But lord, the offense rests in my eyes,
which firmly bar the path of my spirit's flight.[43]
Separation is a flame, my form, a wisp of cotton, 4
and my breath, a breeze that would instantly ignite it,
yet my eyes shed water for their own sake, and so
my body cannot be consumed in the fire of love's
anguish."'
The immensity of Sita's suffering, 5
most merciful one, is better left untold.

31 Treasury of compassion, each moment
passes like an aeon for her,
so go quickly and retrieve her, lord,
routing evildoers with your mighty arms."

1 Learning of Sita's sorrow, the lord of bliss
shed tears from his lotus-like eyes, and asked,
"How can one who totally trusts in me
even dream of knowing such calamity?"
2 Hanuman replied, "Lord, true calamity is only
when you are not recalled and worshiped.
Of what account are these demons, lord?
You will defeat your foes and bring back Janaki."
3 Ram said, "I have no benefactor like you, monkey,
among embodied beings—gods, humans, or sages.
What service can I give you in return?
Before you, my mind can conceive of nothing.[44]
4 No, son, I can never repay my debt to you—
searching my heart, I see this clearly."
Again and again, the savior of gods looked at the monkey
with tear-filled eyes and body flushed with feeling.

32 Hearing the Lord's words and beholding
his face and form, the ecstatic Hanuman
fell at his feet, undone by love,
crying, "Save me, save me, my God!"[45]

1 Though the Lord tried repeatedly to lift him,
he was intoxicated by love and did not care to rise.
The Lord's lovely hand lay on the monkey's head—

recalling that moment, Gauri's lord,* too, sank in bliss.
Then Shankar steadied his mind[46] 2
and resumed telling that most beautiful tale.
Lifting the monkey into his embrace, the Lord
took his hand and seated him right beside him.
"Tell me, monkey, how you managed to burn 3
Ravan's well-guarded Lanka and its mighty stronghold."
Knowing the Lord to be pleased, Hanuman
spoke up, without a trace of pride:
"We branch-dwelling beasts have no greater aim[47] 4
than to jump from one bough to the next.
So if I leaped the ocean, burned a golden city,
slew a horde of night-stalkers, and wrecked a grove—
it all was through your might, Raghu king, 5
and not, master, from any greatness of my own.

Nothing is impossible, lord, for one 33
whom you favor,
for through your glory, a mere wisp of cotton
can incinerate the fire of world's-end![48]

Merciful master, deign to bestow on me devotion 1
that gives bliss and that is firmly enduring."
The Lord heard the monkey's simple words,
Bhavani,† and then said, "So be it."
Shiva added, "One who knows Ram's nature, Uma, 2
never forsakes his worship for any other pursuit,

* Shiva.
† Parvati.

and one whose heart contains this dialogue
attains devotion to the Raghu lord's feet."[49]
3 At the Lord's speech the monkey host cheered—
"Victory to the merciful one, source of bliss!"
Then the Raghu lord summoned the lord of monkeys
and said, "Make ready to march.
4 Why delay any longer now?
Quickly issue orders to your monkeys."
Having seen this spectacle and showered blossoms,
the celestials happily returned to their abodes.[50]

34 The monkey king promptly gave the call,
and his commanders came in crowds
of incomparably mighty monkeys and bears—
a multitude of many hues.

1 Bowing their heads at the Lord's holy feet,
those powerful bears and monkeys roared loudly.
Ram saw that whole army of forest creatures,
and gazed on them benevolently with his lotus eyes.
2 Empowered by Ram's gracious glance, the monkey heroes
became like great mountains endowed with wings.[51]
Then, filled with joy, Ram went forth
as multiple auspicious omens appeared.
3 For when he whose fame abounds in auspiciousness
sets out, it is but right that favorable signs arise.
Vaidehi divined her lord's departure,
for her left limbs trembled, as if telling her of it.
4 But for each propitious sign that Janaki perceived,
a comparable, ominous one appeared to Ravan.

That army departed—and who can ever describe
its countless monkeys and bears, roaring loudly?
Armed with their sharp nails, hefting boulders and trees, 5
they went as they pleased, on earth or in the sky.
They roared like great lions, and the elephants
who support the world staggered and trumpeted.

Those guardians of the quadrants bellowed, earth shook, 6
mountains swayed, and the sea grew turbulent,
but sun and moon, gods, sages, divine serpents,
and demigods inwardly rejoiced, their grief dispelled.[52]
Clashing their teeth in fury, the monkey champions
surged forward in their countless millions
and proclaimed the fame and virtues of Kosala's king:
"Victory to almighty and glorious Lord Ram!"

Unable to endure the burden, 7
the world-bearing serpent king swooned repeatedly,
clutching and deeply scratching with his fangs
the back of the cosmic tortoise, as though,
realizing the supreme splendor
of the Raghu hero's great going-forth,
a snake-king scribe engraved forever
its stainless saga on a tablet of turtle shell.[53]

Proceeding in this way, the sea of mercy 35
descended to the ocean's shore,
where his troops of heroic bears and monkeys
fell to feeding on wild fruits.

1 Meanwhile, the night-stalkers were living uneasily,
ever since a monkey had burned Lanka and left.
Now in every house they all fretted
that their demon race would not be saved.
2 "If he, whose mere messenger's might is indescribable,
himself descends on our city, how will we survive?"
Hearing of the townspeople's talk from female spies,
Queen Mandodari grew utterly distraught.
3 In private, she fell in supplication at her husband's feet,
imploring him in words imbued with prudent counsel:
"Dear husband, abandon your enmity to Lord Hari,
and take my well-meaning words to heart.
4 He whose messenger's awful acts, but recalled,
cause our night-stalkers' wives to miscarry in fear—
summon your ministers and send his own wife
back to him, husband, if you wish our welfare.
5 For it is to afflict the clustered lotuses of your lineage
that Sita has come like a withering winter's night.
Listen to me, lord: if you do not surrender Sita,
not even Shiva or birthless Brahma will help you.

36 Ram's arrows are like a swarm of serpents,
and our night-stalker legions, mere frogs.
So before they devour us all,
give up your obstinacy and take action."

1 The fool's ears listened to her talk, but then
that world-famed egoist burst into laughter:
"How true that women are cowardly by nature—
scared even in security, and mentally immature.

If that pack of monkeys should ever approach, 2
why, my poor hungry demons will feast on them.
That I, in fear of whom the lords of the quadrants quake,
should have a timid wife—what a mighty joke!"
So he declared and, with a laugh, embraced her, 3
and then strode arrogantly off to court.[54]
But Mandodari grew worried in her heart
that fate had turned hostile to her husband.
Seated in his council, Ravan received the news 4
of the enemy's full army reaching the coast.
He asked his ministers to advise him well,
but they all laughed, and said, "Be at ease, lord.
When it was no strain defeating gods and titans, 5
then of what account are men and monkeys?"

Counselor, physician, guru—if this trio 37
lisps pleasing lies from fear or hope of gain,
then realm, religion, and health,
all three rapidly come to ruin.

Such was the counsel contrived for Ravan— 1
mindlessly repeated praise and flattery.
But seizing the moment, Vibhishan entered
and bowed before his elder brother's feet,
then, with head lowered, took his own seat 2
and receiving permission, spoke these words:
"Merciful one, if you ask my advice,
I will speak my mind, brother, for your benefit.
A man who cherishes his own well-being, 3
fame, wisdom, salvation, and all delights,

shuns the face of another man's wife, master,
like the ill-omened moon of the fourth night.[55]
4 For though he be sole master of all fourteen worlds,
one who oppresses beings will not endure,
and if even the most meritorious and urbane man
shows the least covetousness, none speaks well of him.

38 Lust and anger, delusion and avarice—
all these, lord, are highways to hell.
Abandon them all and adore the Raghu hero,
whom saintly ones worship.

1 Dear brother, Ram is no mere human king,
but cosmic sovereign, Death's own demise,
flawless *brahma,* and birthless supreme God,
all-pervading, almighty, without beginning or end.
2 Benefactor of Brahmans, cows, earth, and gods,
that sea of mercy has assumed human form.
He delights the devout and crushes the wicked,
and upholds Veda and dharma, brother.
3 Abandon your enmity to him, and bow down
to the Raghu king, who banishes suppliants' pain.
Return Videha's daughter, master, to that Lord,
and worship Ram, whose love is without motive.
4 The Lord does not spurn one who seeks shelter
even if he incurred the sin of enmity against all.
He whose name effaces the three kinds of pain—
that Lord is now incarnate! Reflect on this, Ravan.

Lord of ten heads, I fall at your feet 39a
time and again and repeat this entreaty:
abandon arrogance, delusion, and pride,
and praise Kosala's great king.

Our grandsire, sage Pulastya, through a pupil, 39b
has sent this same counsel,
and I have promptly conveyed it to you,
dear brother, at this favorable moment."

Now one very wise minister, Malyavan, 1
was delighted by these words and spoke up:
"Your young brother is a jewel of statecraft,
so take Vibhishan's speech to heart!"
But Ravan roared, "These two fools dare extol 2
our enemy. Is there no one here to expel them?"
Then Malyavan withdrew to his abode,
but Vibhishan once again entreated:
"Wisdom and folly abide in all hearts, 3
master—so the *purāṇas* and Veda affirm.
Where there is wisdom, all abundance ensues,
but where folly reigns, the outcome is disaster.
Folly's perversion now dwells in your heart, 4
and you see good for bad, enemy for friend.
She who is the night of death for our demon clan—
Sita—is the object of your mad infatuation!

Brother, clasping your feet I entreat you, 40
out of your affection for me:

give Sita back to Ram,
and you will suffer no harm."

1 In accord with learned ones, *purāṇas,* and Veda,
Vibhishan expounded on prudent policy,
but the ten-headed one leaped up in rage, crying,
"Scoundrel, your death is now imminent!
2 You subsist, always, by my nurture and leave, fool,[56]
yet taking my enemy's side suits your fancy.
Just tell me, traitor, who in all this world
have I not bested with my mighty arms?
3 Yet, living in my city, you fawn on some ascetics—
so go to them, scoundrel, and ply your counsel!"
So saying, he struck him a harsh blow with his foot,
yet his younger brother clung determinedly to it.
4 Shiva said, "Uma, such is the greatness of holy ones,
who return goodness even for mistreatment."[57]
Vibhishan cried, "Like a father, you may well strike me,
yet, lord, your welfare lies in worshiping Ram!"
5 Then with his advisers he rose into the sky,
addressing these words to the assembly:

41 "Lord Ram is avowed to truth
and your court is in the grip of death.
So do not fault me now as I go
to seek refuge with the Raghu hero."

1 As soon as Vibhishan, saying this, departed,
the whole demon clan became doomed.[58]
"Contempt for holy ones, Bhavani," Shiva observed,

"immediately destroys all well-being."
The moment that Ravan expelled Vibhishan, 2
that luckless one lost his regal luster.
But his brother went joyfully to the Raghu king,
his heart astir with many yearnings:
"Now I will behold those pure and lovely feet, 3
tender and lotus-pink, the delight of his servants—
those feet that, with a touch, saved the seer's wife,[59]
and purified the Dandak forest,
the feet that Janak's daughter took into her heart 4
when they trod the earth after the illusory deer,
that float as lotus flowers on Hara's* heart-lake—
it will be my great good fortune to behold.

Those feet, upon whose sandals 42
Bharat subsists with all his heart,
those feet I will now, this very day,
go and behold with these eyes of mine!"

Lovingly musing in this way, 1
he quickly reached the sea's farther shore.
When the monkeys saw Vibhishan approaching,
they took him for a special emissary of the foe.
Detaining him, they went to King Sugriv 2
and reported all the tidings.
Sugriv said, "Raghu king, listen—
Ten-face's brother has come to meet you."
The Lord answered, "What is your opinion, friend?" 3

* Shiva's.

"Ruler of men," said the monkey monarch,
"there is no knowing the evil magic of night-stalkers.
For what purpose has this shape-shifter come?
4 The scoundrel comes to learn our secrets!
To hold him captive would best suit me."
Ram said, "Friend, you strategize correctly,
yet I have vowed to allay the fears of refugees."
5 Hanuman rejoiced to hear the Lord's promise
of tender love to all who seek his divine shelter.

43 "Those who abandon seekers of refuge,
calculating their own potential loss,
are the vilest of people—sinners,
the very sight of whom is harmful.

1 Even one tainted by slaying a billion Brahmans,
if he seeks my shelter, I would not spurn,
for as soon as a soul turns toward me,
sins of millions of births are at once destroyed.
2 The sinful, by their very nature,
never find satisfaction in my worship.
If this one truly had an evil heart,
could he ever have come before me?
3 Only the pure in heart can attain me,
and hypocrisy and duplicity displease me.
Yet even if the ten-headed one sent him to spy,
there is no fear of harm, king of monkeys,
4 for, friend, all the night-stalkers in this world
could be slain by Lakshman in one second.

But if he comes meekly seeking my shelter,
I will cherish him like my own life-breath.

Either way, bring him to me," 44
said the most gracious one with a smile,
and, hailing his mercy, Sugriv set out
together with Angad and Hanuman.

Respectfully placing Vibhishan before them, 1
they went to the Raghu lord, treasury of mercy.
From afar he glimpsed those two brothers
who bestow bliss on the eyes,
then focused on Ram, beauty's paragon, 2
and halted, to gaze with stunned, unblinking eyes
at his long arms, his eyes red as lotuses,
his dark form that frees suppliants of fear,
his lion-like shoulders, lovely broad chest, 3
and countenance that infatuates countless Kamas.
With tear-filled eyes, his whole body thrilling,
Vibhishan composed himself and softly said,
"Lord, I am brother of the ten-faced one, 4
born in the night-stalker race—savior of gods—
base-bodied and as innately addicted to sin
as an owl is enamored of darkness.

Yet my ears heard of your fame, Lord, 45
as destroyer of rebirth's pain, and I came.
Save me, Raghu hero, save me—you who
remove affliction and succor shelter-seekers!"

1 So he spoke, and seeing him fall prostrate,
the Lord at once arose with sheer delight.
His humble speech much pleased the Lord,
and with his great arms, he held him to his heart.
2 Embracing him with Lakshman, he seated him close by
and spoke words to remove his devotee's dread:
"Tell us, lord of Lanka, are you and your family[60]
well, though you dwell in an evil place?
3 Living day and night in the company of the wicked,
how do you adhere to dharma, friend?
Indeed, I know all about your ways—
your wisdom in statecraft and distaste for injustice.
4 One might manage to dwell in hell, brother,
but God spare one the society of the sinful!"
Vibhishan said, "Now that I behold your feet, Raghu king,
I am well, for you mercifully take me as your own.

46 No soul can ever be truly well
or find peace of mind even in dreams,
until it begins to worship Ram,
abandoning desire—sorrow's citadel.

1 The heart remains occupied by many villains—
greed, delusion, envy, arrogance, and pride—
until it houses the master of the Raghus,
bearing bow and arrows, quiver cinched at his waist.
2 Egoism is a night of deep darkness,
delighting the raptor birds of lust and rancor.
It abides in the hearts of all beings
until the sun of the Lord's splendor rises.

I am truly well now, my awful terrors erased 3
when I behold, Ram, your pure and lovely feet.
Merciful one, the one whom you favor
is never pervaded by the three kinds of worldly pain.[61]
I am but a night-stalking demon of basest nature, 4
who has never done any good deeds.
Yet he whose form eludes even meditating sages—
that very Lord has joyfully embraced me!

My good fortune is immeasurable, Ram, 47
treasury of grace and bliss,
to see with my own eyes your lotus-like feet,
eternally worshiped by Shiva and Brahma."

Ram replied, "Friend, I will tell you my own nature, 1
known to Bhushundi, and to Shiva and Girija:*
one who has raged against all beings,
yet meekly comes to me seeking shelter,
relinquishing pride, delusion, and all duplicity,[62] 2
I quickly make the equal of a saintly one.
Mother, father, brother, sons, and wife,
body, fortune, home, friends, and family—
one who weaves all these strands of selfhood 3
into a cord binding his heart to my feet,
who is impartial and free of desire,
and whose mind holds no joy, grief, or fear—
such a good soul abides as securely in my heart 4
as does wealth in that of a miser.

* Parvati.

True ones like you are dear to me,
and I take a body through no other obligation.

48 Worshipers of God with attributes, benevolent
to all, devoted to virtue, firm in vows,
and who adore the feet of the twice-born—
I cherish such ones as my own life's breaths.

1 Lord of Lanka, you own all these merits
and so are exceedingly beloved to me."
Hearing Ram's words, the monkey legions
all cried, "Victory to the treasury of mercy!"
2 Vibhishan heard the Lord's speech
as nectar to his insatiably thirsting ears,
and again and again touched Ram's lovely feet,
with boundless love his heart could not contain.
3 "Divine master of moving and unmoving beings,
guardian of refuge seekers, inner knower of the heart—
my own had harbored certain yearnings,
all swept away by the river of love for your feet.
4 Now, merciful one, grant me pure devotion to you
such that eternally delights Lord Shiva's heart."
"So be it," said the Lord who is steadfast in battle,
and at once he ordered ocean water brought.[63]
5 "Friend, though you have no wish for this,
beholding me unfailingly yields fruit in this world."
And so Ram placed a royal mark on his brow
as a torrent of flowers fell from heaven.

Though he fanned the inferno of Ravan's wrath 49a
with the wind of his own breaths,[64]
Vibhishan was rescued from immolation
and given endless dominion.

The wealth that Shiva had bestowed on Ravan 49b
when he offered up all ten of his heads—
that same fortune the Raghu lord now gave
to Vibhishan as his most modest gift.[65]

One who spurns such a lord to worship any other 1
is but a beast minus tail and horns.
Recognizing his servant, Ram accepted him,
and the Lord's innate nature pleased the monkeys.
Then the omniscient one, indweller of hearts, 2
omnipresent, yet independent and utterly detached,
spoke words that upheld prudent counsel,
having become a man to slay the clan of demons:
"Brave king of monkeys and lord of Lanka, 3
how may this abysmal ocean be traversed?
Swarming with crocodiles, serpents, and fish,
it is most fathomless and formidable to cross."
The lord of Lanka said, "Raghu king, although 4
your arrow can evaporate innumerable oceans,
yet prudent policy dictates that you first
approach the sea and make petition.

Lord, the ocean is linked to your lineage,[66] 50
so he will ponder and propose a plan

to effortlessly bring to his farther shore
all the legions of monkeys and bears."

1 Ram said, "You advise me well, friend,
and so I shall act, if fortune aids us."[67]
But Lakshman was displeased by this counsel,
and Ram's speech greatly saddened him.
2 "What faith is there in 'fortune,' master?
Harden your heart and dry up this ocean!
Fortune and fate are the sole crutch of cowards,
incessantly invoked by the indolent."
3 The Raghu hero heard him, but said with a smile,
"Still, I will proceed thus, so be patient."
So the Lord instructed his young brother;
then the Raghu king repaired to the ocean's edge.
4 First he reverently saluted him, bowing his head,
then sat on sacred grass spread on the shore.
Now, as soon as Vibhishan went to the Lord,
Ravan had sent spies after him.

51 They had witnessed the whole encounter,
deceitfully guised in monkey forms,
and in their hearts, they praised the Lord's virtues
and his love for asylum seekers.

1 But then they openly lauded Ram's nature
with heartfelt love, forgetting their disguises,
and the monkeys knew them for enemy spies
and brought them all, bound, before their king.
2 Sugriv said, "Forest dwellers, hear my command:

beat up these night-stalkers and send them back."
At this order, those monkeys scampered off
and paraded their captives all round the camp.
The monkey troops began thrashing them soundly, 3
even when the poor wretches cried for mercy—
"Those who would deface us will defame
the good name of Kosala's great king!"[68]
Lakshman heard this and summoned them, 4
smiled with compassion, and promptly set them free,
saying, "Put this letter in Ravan's hands, and tell him,
'Read Lakshman's words, scourge of your clan.'

And verbally deliver to that fool 52
my magnanimous message:
'Returning Sita, come before Ram,
or else your doom is sealed.'"

Reverently bowing before Lakshman, 1
the couriers departed, lauding his virtues.
Proclaiming Ram's fame, they came to Lanka
and laid their heads at Ravan's feet.
The ten-faced one snickered and asked their chief, 2
"Won't you tell us how you are, Shuk?
And then, say how fares that Vibhishan,
whose death is now imminent—
that fool who forsook lordship over Lanka 3
to be a wretched worm in grain bound for grinding![69]
Then tell of the bear and monkey brigade,
driven to come here by a cruel fate,
and whose lives are now safeguarded 4

only by that kindly old dolt, Ocean.
And say, what of those two wretched ascetics
whose hearts tremble in dread of me?

53 Did you meet them, or had they already turned back
when their ears heard of my renown?
Speak up! What of the enemy army's mettle and might?
Or have your wits been altogether dazed?"

1 Shuk said, "Lord, as you have graciously inquired,
so heed our report, abandoning your ire.
When your brother went to meet him,
Ram at once adorned his forehead with the royal sign.
2 And when they heard we were Ravan's spies,
the monkeys bound and much tormented us,
even making to bite off our ears and noses,
till we invoked Ram's name and were released.
3 You ask, master, about Ram's army,
but even a billion tongues could not describe
that horde of multihued monkeys and bears,
fierce-faced, gigantic, and terrifying.
4 The one who burned our city and slew your son
is of but trifling might amid all those monkeys—
formidable fighters bearing innumerable names,
huge, and with the strength of countless elephants.

54 There are Dvivid, Mayand, Nil, and Nal,
Angad, Gad, Vikatasya too,
Dadhimukh, Kehari, Nisath, Sath,
and Jambavan—all of awesome might.

All these monkeys are comparable to Sugriv, 1
and there are uncountable millions more like them.
Matchless in might through Ram's favor,
they reckon the three worlds but a wisp of straw!
And I heard, lord of ten necks, 2
that their chiefs alone fill eighteen armies,
and master, there is no monkey in that horde
who cannot defeat you in battle.
Rubbing their hands in utter rage, 3
they all but await the Raghu lord's command,
crying, 'We'll dry up the sea along with its creatures,
or pave it over with mighty mountain peaks!
We'll pound that Ten-head into the dust!'— 4
so all those monkeys declare.
Fearless by nature, they cuss and roar,
as though ready to swallow our Lanka.

Every monkey and bear is a born champion, 55
and at their head is Lord Ram,
who can defeat Death himself, Ravan,
a billionfold on any field![70]

Ram's immense energy, strength, and wisdom 1
cannot be sung by a myriad serpent kings.
With one arrow he could soak up a hundred seas,
yet he judiciously sought your brother's counsel,
and heeding his suggestion, now petitions the sea 2
for safe passage, his mind intent on mercy."
When Ravan heard this, he rocked with laughter—
"If such is his wit, no wonder he made apes his allies!

3 He resolves upon a born coward's counsel,
and places his childish trust in the sea.
Imbecile! You magnify him in vain,
for I have fathomed my foe's intellect and might.
4 With timid Vibhishan for an adviser,
where on earth can he find victory and fame?"
That villain's railing vexed the messenger,
who judged the time right to produce the letter.
5 "Ram's younger brother gave me this message—
read it, master, and cool your ire."
Ravan guffawed and took it with his left hand;[71]
then the rogue called a minister to read it out:

56a "Scoundrel, do not let flattering words
beguile your mind and wreck your race.
If you stand opposed to Ram, you will find
no haven even with Vishnu, Brahma, and Shiva.

56b Either renounce pride and be like your brother—
a bee resting on the Lord's lotus feet—
or else, villain, with your family, fall like moths
into the flames of Ram's arrows."

1 Frightened at heart, yet outwardly smiling,
ten-headed Ravan declared to the assembly:
"Face down in the dust, yet reaching for the sky—
how the little mendicant's mouth runs over!"
2 Shuk replied, "Master, his words are entirely true.
Shed your innate pride and realize this.
Relinquish your rage and hear me out,

lord—abandon your enmity toward Ram.
The Raghu hero is most tender by nature, 3
though he reigns over all the worlds.
When once you meet him, the Lord will be kind
and keep not one of your faults in mind.
Return Janak's daughter to the Raghu master, 4
lord. Act on at least this much of my advice."
But when Shuk spoke of surrendering Vaidehi,*
that scoundrel struck him with his foot.
Shuk merely bowed to him, then flew straight 5
to the sea of mercy, the Raghu master.
Saluting him, he recounted his own story
and by Ram's grace regained his previous state—
for you see, Bhavani, by the seer Agastya's curse 6
he had become a demon, though he was a wise adept.
Then, singing the praises of Ram's feet,
that sage set out for his own hermitage.

Meanwhile, the dumb sea did not heed supplication, 57
though three days had passed.
Then Ram spoke in wrath:
"Unless frightened, he will not show us favor.

Lakshman, bring my quiver and bow— 1
I will dry up the sea with a fiery arrow!
To petition a fool or befriend a swindler,
or preach generosity to an innate miser,
to tell wise tales to the self-obsessed, 2

* Sita.

or to expound detachment to the covetous,
calm to the enraged, or Hari's story to the lustful—
is all as fruitful as sowing seed on a sandbar."
3 So saying, the Raghu lord lifted his bow—
this new tack much pleased Lakshman—
and affixed an awesome arrow.
Then in the ocean's bosom a fire arose,
4 tormenting its hosts of reptiles and fish.
When the sea god saw his creatures burning,
he heaped a golden platter with coral and gems
and came in Brahman guise, forsaking his pride.

58 "Though one water it incessantly, a plantain
only yields its fruit when pruned," said Bhushundi.
"Just so, king of birds, the crude do not heed courtesy,
and bow only upon rebuke."

1 Frightened, Ocean fell at the Lord's feet,
saying, "Master, forgive all my flaws!
Sky, wind, fire, water, and earth
all function out of innate insentience.
2 Inspired by you, Maya spawned us
for creation's sake—so all the holy books declare.
And as and to whomever the Lord mandates,
one rests content only in abiding by that order.
3 You acted rightly, Lord, to chastise me,
though you yourself have ordained my limits.
Drum, rustic, Shudra, beast, and woman
are all deserving of beating.[72]
4 By your fiery brilliance, Lord, I can be dried up

and your army can cross—but my stature will suffer.[73]
Your command is inexorable, as the Veda declares,
so let me quickly do whatever will please you."

Hearing this most humble speech, 59
the compassionate one smiled and said,
"Revered elder, tell us the means by which
our army of monkeys can cross over."

"Master, two monkey brothers, Nil and Nal, 1
in youth were blessed by a seer," Ocean said,
and at their mere touch huge boulders
will float on the sea—because of your glory!
I too, Lord, bearing your majesty on my breast, 2
will assist in accordance with my powers.
Have the sea subdued, master, in such a way
that your fame may be sung in the three worlds,
and redirect this arrow of yours to my northern shore, 3
to slay the evil sinners dwelling there."[74]
When merciful Ram heard of Ocean's inner pain,
he removed it at once, for he is resolute in battle.
Seeing Ram's immense strength and heroism, 4
happy Ocean, the abode of waters, grew contented.
He reported to the Lord of all those misdeeds,[75]
then bowed at his feet and departed.

Ocean returned to his own abode, 5
and the Raghu lord was pleased by his counsel.
This noble saga, that purges the filth of the Kali Age,
servant Tulsi has sung according to his understanding.

An abode of bliss, quelling doubt and destroying grief—
such are the myriad virtues of the Raghu prince.
Forsaking every other hope and faith—
foolish mind—recite and listen to them unceasingly.

The singing of Lord Raghu's virtues
bestows all blessings,
and those who listen reverently will cross,
without a boat, the sea of worldly rebirth.

[The end of the fifth stair of the *Rāmcaritmānas,*
which annihilates all impurities of the Kali Age.]

# NOTES TO THE TRANSLATION

*In the Forest*

1 Like other sub-books of the *Mānas,* this one opens with an "auspicious invocation" (*maṅgalācaraṇa*) consisting of several verses in Sanskrit. Their marginal numbering precedes that of the Hindi text, which begins with the couplet in *soraṭhā* meter numbered "0."

2 "Of Brahma's lineage," *brahmakulaṃ;* this unusual identification of Shiva, though semantically straightforward, has generated many interpretations among *Mānas* commentators (see *Mānaspīyūṣ* 5.1.3–4). It might refer to a puranic tradition that Rudra (Shiva's aggressive alter ego) was born from Brahma's frown.

3 The vocative "Uma" signals, once again, Shiva's narration to Parvati. Most commentators take this verse to be a reminder of the confusion she experienced, as Sati, when she encountered Ram and Lakshman in the forest during the events being recounted in this sub-book (see *The Epic of Ram, Volume 1,* pp. 109–141 and *Rāmcaritmānas* 1.48–65). Since I follow the common practice of numbering *Mānas* stanzas by the couplets with which they end, this introductory one is assigned "0."

4 In the *Vālmīki Rāmāyaṇa,* the incident is described in *Sundarakāṇḍa* by Sita to Hanuman, as an intimate episode known only to herself and Ram, so that Hanuman may verify to Ram that he has truly seen Sita (5.36.12–33; Goldman and Goldman 1996: 216–218). In that version the crow pecks Sita's breast, likewise drawing blood.

5 When this notoriously irritable sage once attempted to curse King Ambarisha, a devotee of Vishnu, his curse provoked Sudarshan, Vishnu's razor-sharp discus, to pursue the sage to the ends of the earth, until Durvasa ultimately fell at the feet of his intended victim and begged for mercy. The story, found in *Bhāgavatapurāṇa* 9.4.2.218.4, is twice alluded to by Tulsidas in *Ayodhyākāṇḍ* (see 2.218.4 and 2.265.2).

6 The invocation of Garuda—here identified as "Hari's mount" (*harijānā*)—signals that the speaker of this aside (appropriately,

within a tale about a crow's misdeed) is now the immortal crow Kak Bhushundi.

7 The vocative once again signals that Shiva is now narrating.

8 "Ears," *śruti;* since this can mean both "ear" and the aurally received Veda, an alternate translation would be that Ram "did countless deeds, like the nectar of the Vedas."

9 The dozen verses that follow are in Sanskrit. Evoking the knowledge of a Brahman sage, they mark a break from the standard poetic register of the *Mānas*. Like other compositions of the genre called *stuti* ("litany of praise"), they are for the most part grammatically simple, though their difficult compounds and sometimes obscure mythological allusions and metaphysical terminology, evoking the knowledge of a Brahman sage, mark a break from the standard poetic register of the *Mānas.* For detailed theological analysis, see *Mānaspīyūṣ* 5.1.38–52.

10 In a popular myth, Mount Mandar served as the churning rod when the gods and their demonic cousins churned the cosmic ocean of milk to obtain the nectar of immortality.

11 Shachi is the wife of Indra, king of the Vedic deities. In some theogonies, Vishnu is said to be the younger brother of Indra. This identification may also allude to Vishnu's fifth incarnation as the dwarf Brahman Vamana, who, like Indra, has Aditi as his mother, and who frees Indra and the other gods from the tyranny of the demon Bali.

12 *Turīya* is literally "the fourth state" and refers to a condition that transcends the tripartite created universe; *kevala* (literally "alone") refers to God's independence of creation.

13 "By misguided yogis," *kuyoginā;* this compound, which can simply mean "bad yogis," may be interpreted in various ways. To most *Mānaspīyūṣ* commentators, it implies those who practice yoga for selfish ends, without devotion to Ram (5.1.47).

14 The presence of a final verse extolling the benefits of reciting the preceding Sanskrit *stuti*—a device referred to as *phalaśruti,* or "hearing of the fruits [of recitation]"—further marks this passage for potential liturgical use.

15 "Benefactor," *hitakārī;* since this word can also mean "friend," some interpret the verse as listing four persons whose beneficence to a woman is of a limited nature.

16 Most commentators interpret this, in light of the lines that follow,

to mean that service to a husband yields the highest spiritual reward to a woman.

17 Yama, god of death, presides over an underworld in which souls are punished for misdeeds committed during earthly life.

18 "Faithful wife," *patibratā* (literally, "pledged to a husband"); a conventional designation for a wife who is chaste and also observant of religious rites beneficial to her husband.

19 "A most dreadful hell," *raurava naraka;* although the adjective means "dreadful, formidable," many commentators identify this as the name of one of the twenty-eight hells enumerated in certain *purāṇas.* Here (according to *Mānaspīyūṣ* 5.1.65, note 1) souls are bitten on all sides by tiny vipers.

20 "Inherently," *sahaja* (from birth, naturally); commentators identify the menstrual cycle as the cause of women's impurity. The sacred basil plant (here identified by the alternate name *tulsikā*) is personified as a goddess who (like Lakshmi) is wed to Vishnu. Some commentators prefer to read the phrase "praised in the four Vedas" as referring to the previous line's statement of wifely duty.

21 "Sanak and the sages," *Sanakādi* ("Sanak and so forth"); a reference to four sages who are eternally in the form of young boys.

22 Lakshmi, who is born out of the cosmic ocean when it is churned by the gods and demons, promptly chooses Vishnu as her spouse.

23 No verb is given, but I agree with commentators who take what follows as Atri's inner reflection.

24 Since this theologically portentous *caupāī* verse virtually repeats one found in the previous sub-book (see *Rāmcaritmānas* 2.123.1 and its note, in volume 3 of *The Epic of Ram*), commentators focus on the substitution of "Shri" for "Sita" in its second occurrence; see *Mānaspīyūṣ* 5.1.80–82.

25 Tulsi's terse account contrasts with the protracted struggle between this horrific demon and Ram and Lakshman depicted in the *Vālmīki Rāmāyaṇa* (3.2–3; Pollock 1991: 89–92). After being slain by the brothers, he reveals that he is actually a *gandharva* (heavenly musician) who was under a curse, and he is able to return to the celestial realm. Tulsi, however, specifies that Ram granted him a place in Ram's own heaven.

26 The sage alludes to Ram's "pledge" (*pana*) to bestow his grace on those who love him wholeheartedly.

27 Tulsi specifies that Sharabhang was given a place in Vaikunth, the

heavenly realm where Vishnu is said to reside. He further explains that this was owing to the sage's prior request for "devotion-in-separation" (*bheda bhagati,* or "devotion with [awareness of] difference"), which many Vaishnavas consider to be a dualistic ultimate state more desirable than the Advaita goal of union with the Absolute.

28 Although the four-armed form is the divine manifestation in which Vishnu commonly appears, Tulsi implies that a true devotee of Ram prefers to see him embodied as a human prince. Ram deprives the sage of this vision, substituting the conventional Vishnu form, to bring him out of his devotional trance and permit him to enjoy Ram's actual, physical presence. The simile refers to the belief that king cobras possess, in their hoods, a magical gem.

29 "Garbed as an ascetic," *paridhana municīraṃ;* literally, "(wearing) a lower garment of cloth used by ascetics." This *caupāī* verse begins a series of seven that are grammatically in Sanskrit, after which Sutikshan continues his homage in a mixed language that combines the standard Avadhī dialect of the epic with several Sanskrit forms.

30 "Foe of Khar," *kharāri;* this epithet shows poetic anachronism or saintly prescience, since Ram will not encounter the demon Khar until 3.18.1.

31 "Pride," *abhimāna;* this word generally has negative connotations for Tulsi, who routinely lists it among the sins that plague human beings. Hence its valuation here in a devotional context is striking.

32 *Mānas* scholars disagree on whether the adjective "desireless" (*nihakāma*), placed at the end of the verse, refers to the sage's heart or to Ram as the moon. Those favoring the latter interpretation observe that Ram, though without desires, will accede to the wish of a devotee, or else gloss it as "stable, unmoving," and hence as referring to a constant moon that does not wax, wane, or transit the sky (see *Mānaspīyūṣ* 5.1.120–122).

33 The conventional sense of this half verse seems to be, "I will not be any inconvenience to you." But by thus inviting himself to accompany the brothers and Sita, the sage is (as the next line suggests) using an ingenious ruse that shows devotional "cleverness" (*caturāī*) to maximize his own enjoyment of Ram's company via the pretext of visiting his guru. Some commentators also explain that Agastya had, long ago, asked Sutikshan to bring Ram to him as his "guru fee" (*guru dakṣiṇā*), and hence the

allusion to "no obligation" obliquely refers to the pupil's debt to his teacher.

34 *Śarad* is the season that follows the rains and is characterized by cloudless skies in which the moon, beloved by *cakor* birds, appears with particular clarity.

35 "Sacred counsel," *mantra;* in this context, commentators gloss this as "counsel, advice," but it can also imply a sacred formula to activate supernatural weapons to be deployed against demons, such as Agastya bestows on Ram in the *Adhyātmarāmāyaṇa* (3.3.45–46; Chhawchharia 2010: 1.295).

36 "Wild fig tree," *ūmari taru;* this type of fig (also known as *gūlar*) is known for the abundant clusters of fruit that appear on its trunk.

37 "Panchavati," *pañcabaṭī;* "place of five banyan trees." Contemporary devotees identify it with a place along the Godavari River, near Nasik in Maharashtra state.

38 The *Mānaspīyūṣ* cites two traditions about the cursing of this forest tract. In one ("for which no written source is available"), sage Gautam curses it because of a deception practiced on him by a group of ascetics who dwell there. In the other, said to be recounted in the *Padmapurāṇa* as well as in the *Vālmīki Rāmāyaṇa,* Shukracharya, guru of the gods, curses the kingdom of Raja Dand after the latter rapes the guru's daughter. Both stories are recounted in the context of Tulsi's first mention of the Dandak forest, in *Bālkāṇḍ* (1.24.4; see *Mānaspīyūṣ* 1.385–386).

39 "Vulture king," *gīdharāja;* this is Jatayu, an aged, semidivine bird of a species of carrion eaters traditionally regarded as extremely vile. The story of his longtime friendship with Ram's father that he extends to his son as soon as Ram identifies himself is found in Valmiki's epic (3.13; Pollock 1991: 115–117).

40 The dialogue that follows (through *dohā* verse 16) is often referred to by commentators as the *Rām gītā,* recalling Krishna's battlefield sermon to Arjuna, the *Bhagavadgītā.* It parallels a similar didactic passage at roughly the same point in the narrative in *Adhyātmarāmāyaṇa* (3.4.18–55; Chhawchharia 2010: 1.299–313).

41 "Occult powers," *siddhi:* supernatural abilities acquired through the practice of asceticism and yoga; "triple qualities," *tīni guna:* the three constituent properties of all created things according to Samkhya philosophy—lucidity (*sattva*), passion (*rajas*), and darkness (*tamas*).

42 I use "God" to translate two different words in this couplet, *īsa* and *sīva*. Both seem to refer, here, to the personified Supreme Being, but the second one, used to rhyme with *jīva* ("the soul"), is notably also a form of Shiva's name. This *dohā* verse, identified by some commentators as the essence of Ram's discourse, has generated abundant interpretation; see *Mānaspīyūṣ* 5.1.164–169.

43 "Devotion," *bhagati;* literally "participation," "sharing"—understood as sharing in the divine and in expressions of loving worship.

44 "Brahman seers," *bipra;* this archaic word originally referred to the seers (*ṛṣis*) who first uttered the Vedic mantras. By Tulsi's time, it had become synonymous with the Brahman caste, and that is how most commentators interpret it. "One's proper work," *nija karma;* the implication is of following the occupation and way of life prescribed by the social rank into which one is born.

45 "Ninefold devotion," *nava bhakti;* many Vaishnava texts describe nine steps on the devotional path—one of which is "listening" (to stories of the Lord)—though they do not always fully agree on the nature or sequence of these steps. Influential descriptions of them are found in the *Bhāgavatapurāṇa* (7.5.23–24) and later in this sub-book, when Ram expounds them to the ascetic woman Shabari (3.35.4–36.3).

46 "Master," *pati;* this may also be translated "husband" or "lord."

47 "Shurpanakha," *sūpanakhā;* from the Sanskrit *śūrpanakhā,* "she whose nails are (as big as) winnowing fans."

48 "Garuda," *uragārī;* literally, "foe of snakes"; this vocative, an epithet of the divine eagle who feeds on serpents, again signals that the narrator, at least of this aside, is the crow Bhushundi.

49 "Sunstone," *rabimani;* this is identified by commentators as a "solar gem" (*sūryakānt maṇi*), often translated as jasper or "sun ruby." The *Mānaspīyūṣ* admits to being unable to locate any lore according to which this stone "melts" or emits liquid when heated by the sun, although there is a tradition that it may emit fire. In any case, the simile signals an involuntary response to an external stimulus, which suits the maxim. Regarding the message of the latter, many commentators maintain that the word "woman" here (*nārī*) refers only to a "wicked" female like Shurpanakha, and not to women in general (see *Mānaspīyūṣ* 5.1.199–203).

50 "Bachelor," *kuāra;* although this word can simply mean "a youth,"

its implication in the context is of an unmarried young man. As in the Valmiki text, Ram's utterance of an apparent falsehood (since Lakshman is in fact married to Urmila, Sita's half sister) has occasioned copious commentary; see *Mānaspīyūṣ* 5.1.207–209.

51 The implication, apparently, is that Ram can take another wife if he chooses.

52 There is disagreement among traditional scholars as to both the text and meaning of the final example given by Lakshman, with some favoring "a spy craving virtues" (*cāra gunānī*). The common expression "to draw milk from the sky" refers to desiring something that is impossible.

53 Some manuscripts and printed editions of the *Mānas* join or hyphenate these two names, and some commentators treat them as referring to a single demon. See, however, 1.14d, which suggests that Tulsi regards them as a fraternal pair.

54 In this verse in *harigītikā chand* meter, Ram's dark, "bluish" complexion is likened to emerald and his arms to snakes. The long matted locks of ascetics, treated with the sap of the banyan, may become bleached by the sun and show reddish-yellow streaks, inviting the lightning simile.

55 A category of celestial demons called *mandeh* are said to daily attack the rising sun, but are driven off as he grows brighter and stronger, fortified (according to some commentators) by the mantra-charged water offered by pious Hindus during their sunrise rituals; see *Mānaspīyūṣ* 5.1.226.

56 Such lists of weaponry will recur in later battle scenes, especially in sub-book six. Many of the names refer to specialized, archaic weapons no longer familiar to modern readers, and the *Mānaspīyūṣ* provides detailed definitions (5.1.231); I offer English approximations.

57 "Hissing," *phuṅkarata* (literally, "puffing"); this refers to a sound that king cobras make when aroused and prepared to strike.

58 The third demon brother is Trishira (*triśirā*, "three heads"), who has not been mentioned previously.

59 "Iron-tipped arrows," *nārāca;* according to the *Mānaspīyūṣ*, a special type of arrow made of iron "with five fins attached [to the shaft] and four to the arrowhead. Its impact is very terrible" (5.1.234).

60 "Vampiric spirits," *betāla;* this is a category of malevolent spirit sometimes said to reanimate corpses and drink the blood of the

living. The term *joginī,* though literally meaning "a female yogi," refers to a class of wild, voracious demigoddesses who haunt battlefields and cremation grounds to feast on corpses.

61 Commentators note that their cries consisted of ejaculations such as "There's Ram; kill him!" Nevertheless, by the power of Ram's name, all attained the state of *nirbāna,* which is glossed here as "liberation" (*mokṣa*).

62 "Annihilation," *dhuā̃;* in modern Hindi this means "smoke," but here it is evidently a premodern idiom possibly alluding to the smoke of cremation and signifying "rack and ruin," "utter destruction."

63 "Offered to Lord Hari," *harihi samarpe;* ironically, the enraged Shurpanakha offers proverbial and pious advice, even invoking Vishnu as God.

64 "Most lovely young woman," *syāmā;* literally, "dark woman." This word is the feminine form of one of dark-skinned Krishna's epithets, and hence also a name of his beloved, Radha. Other passages, however, imply that Sita is light-skinned, and commentators conventionally gloss this term as "a beautiful, youthful maiden."

65 "Base form," *tāmasa dehā;* literally, "body of darkness or inertia." *Rākṣasas* and other demonic beings are said to be constituted primarily of this fundamental cosmic quality.

66 With this vocative, Tulsi calls attention to the fact that the brief "secret" narrative that follows (until the story of Ravan's visit to Marich resumes in the middle of *caupāī* verse 3.24.3) is disclosed by Shiva to Parvati. The story of Sita's entry into fire and her substitution of a simulacrum (*pratibimba:* "shadow, likeness, reflection")—evidently to spare her the indignity of Ravan's touch—was previously told in the *Adhyātmarāmāyaṇa* (3.7.1–4; Chhawchharia 2010: 1.336–337).

67 Each of these motions betokens an aggressive act (thus, the bent or lowered goad will strike an elephant's head, the cat bends before pouncing on its prey, and so forth).

68 Literally, "for at his killing, (one) dies, at his giving life, (one) lives."

69 Marich first appeared in the poem as one of the demons who tried to disrupt Sage Vishvamatra's fire sacrifice; see *The Epic of Ram, Volume 1,* p. 111 and *Rāmcaritmānas* 1.210.1–2.

70 "Predatory wasp," *bhṛnga;* a type of wasp believed to seize other insects and carry them away (as Ram's arrow did with Marich), and

also to bewitch them so that they become enamored of or obsessed with their captor (as the next half line implies).

71 According to the *Mānaspīyūṣ*, this proverb-like enumeration of individuals who might prove harmful to one is based on a Sanskrit verse found in *Cāṇakyanīti* (Worldly wisdom of Chanakya), a collection of aphorisms attributed to the same ancient author who reputedly composed the famous treatise on statecraft, *Arthaśāstra*. For the last item in the series, "clever cook" (*bhānasa gunī*), some early manuscripts read *mānasa gunī*, which commentators gloss as "astrologer" or "soothsayer" (*Mānaspīyūṣ* 5.1.271).

72 "Wholly independent," *abasahi;* literally, "without (external) control." However, an alternative reading ("but whom devotion assuredly sways") is possible, since *abasahi* may also mean "assuredly," "undoubtedly" (modern Hindi, *avaśya*). This verse is in lyrical *harigītikā* meter.

73 "Faithful to his vows," *satyasandha;* according to the *Mānaspīyūṣ*, this refers less to Ram's vow to slay demons than to his promise, at the time of their marriage, to do what would please Sita; see *Mānaspīyūṣ* 5.1.278.

74 "Stinging words," *marama bacana;* also "secret, penetrating speech." Tulsi merely alludes here to the caustic speech recorded in the Valmiki epic, in which Sita accuses Lakshman of disloyalty to his brother and of having sexual designs on her (*Rāmāyaṇa* 3.43; Pollock 1991: 176–179). Citing this, the *Mānaspīyūṣ* compiler remarks, "That which our revered poet, knowing it to be improper, did not write, this humble one is unable to quote. Those who wish may look it up" (5.1.287).

75 The vocative identifying Garuda signals that this aside is spoken by the crow Bhushundi, one of Tulsi's four narrators (though his name does not appear in the verse).

76 In this provocative juxtaposition, the motive behind Ravan's inner reverence and pleasure (which seems contradicted by the *dohā* verse that follows) has elicited many interpretations from commentators—such as admiration for Sita's beauty and spirit, devotion to her as supreme goddess, or satisfaction at the confirmation of his hunch that he will gain a blessed death at her husband's hands. See *Mānaspīyūṣ* 5.1.295–296.

77 "Gods' portion," *puroḍāsa;* a special oblation offered as part of a Vedic fire sacrifice.

78 "Mainak," a flying mountain; "king of birds," Garuda, Vishnu's mount.

79 Some commentators prefer, "remembering Ram and having done wondrous deeds." This is possible since the word *kari* can be either a conjunctive participle ("having done") or a genitive postposition ("his," here, "Ram's").

80 "Grove of *aśoka* trees," *bana asoka;* the name of Ravan's palace garden in which Sita is imprisoned identifies it as containing evergreen trees of a species that has ancient religious associations on the subcontinent and is considered auspicious. Its name, ironically in Sita's context, is said to mean "without sorrow."

81 That is, Ravan arranged for Sita to be guarded and further harassed by demon women.

82 The list of items that follows is each conventionally likened, in Indian poetry, to features of a beautiful woman's body. Thus, the wagtail, deer, and fish are cited for their large, lustrous eyes, the parrot for its beak (likened to a well-formed nose), the dove for its graceful neck, the cuckoo for its sweet voice, the serpent for its black, lustrous body (likened to a hair plait), jasmine for its whiteness (likened to teeth), pomegranate for its lip-like redness, Varuna's snare and Kama's bow for their graceful curvature (the bow commonly likened to eyebrows), the *haṃsa* and elephant for their full-hipped gait, the lion for its narrow waist, the wood apple (*bel*) for its round, firm fruit (likened to breasts), gold for its brightness, and so on. In citing each of these, Ram implies that, since Sita's beautiful features surpass theirs in every respect, they must now be reveling in her absence ("they hear themselves praised"—that is, in their own right, rather than as metaphors for feminine charms). In addition, as commentators observe, this list indirectly and subtly offers a kind of "head-to-foot" (*nakha śikha*) description of Sita's beauty from the lips of her anguished husband—a description that the poet has elsewhere modestly refrained from providing (see *Mānaspīyūṣ* 5.1.319–321).

83 The soles of the feet of Vishnu and his human avatars are said to bear certain auspicious marks (often twenty-four in number) in the shape of lotus, goad, pennant, and so on (for a full catalog, see *Mānaspīyūṣ* 5.1.323–324).

84 "Curlew," *kurarī;* commentators identify this name with several species of small, shore-dwelling birds with shrill voices.

85 "My abode," *mama dhāmā;* in Vaishnava eschatology, this is

understood as a heavenly city or landscape imbued with the character of a beloved avatar, usually Ram or Krishna.

86 The remainder of this stanza consists of four quatrains (each comprising eight lines in this translation) in a lyrical meter (technically called ***harigītikā chand***) that Tusidas periodically uses at moment of high emotion or to create an auspicious tableau for meditation.

87 "To whom the desireless are dear," ***akāmapriya***. This can also mean "you who are dear to those without desire."

88 The dark limbs of Vishnu and his human avatars, Krishna and Ram, offset by their characteristic yellow garments, are often poetically likened to the shiny black and yellow banding of the giant honey bee native to South Asia.

89 "Lakshmi's beloved lord," ***ramānivāsa;*** incorporating the feminine form of Ram's own name (***ramā***), this connotes "the abode of Lakshmi" and is a common epithet of Vishnu.

90 Kabandh was a heavenly musician (*gandharva*) who was cursed to become a headless monster with immense arms and a gaping maw in his belly, into which he stuffed whatever creatures he could capture. When he seized Ram and Lakshman, the two heroes severed his arms, which began his release from the curse (see the *Vālmīki Rāmāyaṇa* 3.65–69; Pollock 1991: 229–240). In several versions of the story, Kabandh was deformed by Indra or through the curse of the sage Ashtavakra, but Tulsi attributes the curse to the irascible Brahman Durvasa.

91 The name Shabari refers to a woman of a forest-dwelling tribe, whose members were regarded as highly impure outcastes by Brahman legalists. A disciple of the sage Matanga, Shabari is instructed by him, when he ascends to heaven, to remain in his ashram and await a visit from Ram (see the *Vālmīki Rāmāyaṇa* 3.70.9–13; Pollock 1991: 241). Ram's acceptance of Shabari's food in the next ***dohā*** verse omits the well-known detail, found in many retellings and in visual art, that Shabari had pretasted each wild berry to ensure its sweetness, and thus further polluted it with her saliva (see Lutgendorf 2000). However, some commentators argue that Tulsi alludes to this in calling the fruits "juiciest" (***surasa ati***); see *Mānaspīyūṣ* 5.1.351.

92 "Events of my story," ***mama kathā prasaṅgā;*** the word ***prasaṅga*** ("topic" or "subject") is conventionally used for individual narrative episodes in an epic story.

93 "Lovely" substitutes here for the conventional (but awkward in English) *karibaragāminī* ("having the gait of a fine elephant"), describing a woman with ample thighs.

94 That is, she tells the story of her guru's order to remain in the ashram and await Ram's coming, or (according to some) the story of Sugriv's enmity with his brother and resultant exile.

95 The *ḍhek* is a long-beaked aquatic bird; the *mahokh,* a brown-headed, crow-size bird that frequents bushes and bamboo thickets. Both are said to have harsh cries.

96 "Fourfold army," *caturaṅginī sena.* A royal army traditionally consisted of units of elephants, cavalry, chariots, and foot soldiers.

97 "Web of magic," *Indrajāla* (literally, "Indra's net"); "conjurer," *naṭa.* The former term is commonly used for the illusions created by magicians, hence in this context, the latter term (which can also mean "actor" or "dancer," as in Shiva's own epithet *naṭarāja,* "king of dancers") suggests a street-performing illusionist.

98 The story of the immortal sage Narad's infatuation with an illusory princess and his subsequent cursing of Vishnu appears in *Bālkāṇḍ;* see 1.125–139 (in volume 1 of *The Epic of Ram*).

99 See *The Epic of Ram, Volume 1,* pp. 255–279 and *Rāmcaritmānas* 1.125.1–139.

100 The implication is that a person's own inner strength, on which a wisdom seeker (*gyānī*) relies, might fail in the face of these foes, whereas that of Ram is infallible.

101 The changing weather and vegetation associated with the traditional "six seasons" of the Indian calendar are metaphorically invoked in this passage, though some of the seasonal names have no apt English translation. After "spring" (*basanta,* roughly March–April), "summer" (*grīṣama,* May–June), and "the rains" (*varaṣā,* July–September), "autumn" is offered for the postmonsoon season of *śarada* (roughly corresponding to October–November), associated with clear and cooler weather and the moonlit nights thought to be beneficial to the *kumuda,* a type of lily. Early winter (*hima,* roughly December–January) follows, which can bring severe cold and even frost. This is followed by still-cool *śiśira* (February–March, "early spring" in my translation), when the tall, tough weed called *javās,* or "camel thorn," proliferates. When this set of seasonal similes ends in verse four, the poet turns to other comparisons.

102 "Six sins," *ṣata bikāra;* commentators provide varying lists of these. The Gita Press gloss offers "lust, anger, greed, delusion, pride, and envy." For other reckonings, see *Mānaspīyūṣ* 5.1.405.

103 A comparable Sanskrit colophon, reminding readers of the allegory of Lake Manas with its ghats and stairways, traditionally closes each book of the epic. It is found in some manuscripts and has become standard in printed editions.

*The Kingdom of Kishkindha*

1 The first two verses are the traditional *maṅgalācaraṇa,* or invocation in Sanskrit. The Avadhī text begins with the pair of couplets in *soraṭhā* meter, likewise invocatory, numbered "0" here since they begin rather than end a stanza.

2 This invocation of the pilgrimage city of Kashi (*kāśī,* "the effulgent"; also called Banaras and Varanasi) is generally assumed to indicate that Tulsidas, by this point in the composition of the epic, had taken up residence there. Appropriately, it is followed by a couplet in praise of Shiva, the city's patron deity.

3 The reference is to the world-threatening venom, called *halāhala,* that was produced as a by-product of the churning of the cosmic ocean to obtain the nectar of immortality. To neutralize it, Shiva drank it, and it turned his throat blue.

4 This may also be read, "If they are wicked-minded and sent by Bali"—that is, by Sugriv's hostile elder brother.

5 In many puranic myths, Lord Vishnu (Narayan) is paired with a dear companion or brother named Nar (literally, "man," "human being").

6 Like other vocative asides in the text, this remark to Uma (Parvati) reminds us that Shiva is narrating this section. However, to some it also signals Shiva's personal "memory" of the episode, since Hanuman is widely believed to be his avatar. For extended discussion of Hanuman's unexplained "recognition" of Ram, implying foreknowledge of his divinity (including the charming story of his service, as a pet monkey, to the child Ram), see *Mānaspīyūṣ* 5.2.25–28 and Lutgendorf 2007: 136–137, 192–194.

7 This extraordinary, emotional assertion has generated many interpretations; see *Mānaspīyūṣ* 5.2.34–36.

8 Although modern visual art often depicts an anthropomorphized Hanuman bearing Ram and Lakshman on his shoulders, one of

my mentors in Banaras, Ramji Pande, dismissed such images as "fanciful" and observed that monkeys proceed on all fours and can carry things only on their backs, as Tulsi explicitly describes.

9 This seemingly straightforward account has produced voluminous commentary, since a traditional Hindu wife does not normally utter her husband's name; for various interpretations, see *Mānaspīyūṣ* 5.2.47–49. According to the *Vālmīki Rāmāyaṇa,* Sita had dropped several of her ornaments, wrapped in a silk shawl (3.52.2–3; Pollock 1991: 201).

10 The name of this *asura* (Maya, with short vowels), who is commonly identified as the chief architect of the demons, should not be confused with the word for cosmic illusion (*māyā*), though both derive from the same Sanskrit verb root meaning to measure, mark off, fashion, form, and so on (Monier-Williams 1960: 804). His son's name, Māyāvī, means "illusionist" or "sorcerer."

11 "A true friend" (*santa mitra*); as commentators note, this can equally be read as "such ... are the qualities of the saintly and of a friend."

12 "Dealt with them," *ḍhahāe;* literally "demolished them." This is Tulsi's terse summary of incidents, often told at greater length in other Ramayanas, in which Sugriv displays doubt concerning Ram's ability to slay Bali and tries to assay the human prince's strength. First Sugriv shows him the mountain-like bones of Dundhubhi, a demon once slain by Bali; with just his big toe, Ram effortlessly kicks these to a great distance. His doubts still not allayed, Sugriv then shows him a line of sturdy trees (according to Valmiki, *śāla,* but in the *Adhyātmarāmāyaṇa* identified as *tāla,* or palmyra palms) that Bali is said to have shaken. Ram responds by firing a single arrow that pierces all seven of their stout trunks. See the *Vālmīki Rāmāyaṇa* account at 4.11.47–52, 4.12.1–5; Lefeber 1994: 77–78.

13 The implication is that Sugriv's speech, imbued with world-weary detachment (*birāga sañjuta*) indicates only a temporary resolve, and that he will soon resume wanting his brother's death and the restoration of his wife and kingdom, which Ram has promised him.

14 This abrupt aside, which the vocative identifies as delivered by the crow Bhushundi to the divine eagle Garuda, is a typical reminder of the multiple dialogues that constitute the *Mānas.* Here it underscores Ram's greater purpose in cooling Sugriv's sudden

impulse toward world renunciation: to launch the search for Sita and hasten Ravan's demise.

15 "With my master," *sanātha;* this literal reading of a term that is sometimes rendered "protected" or even (in a context like this) spiritually "saved" seems appropriate here. Most commentators interpret this to mean that Bali anticipates salvation through dying at Ram's hands.

16 Typically the *harigītikā chand* meter, present in the eight lines that follow this *caupāī* verse preceding *dohā* verse 10, breaks the flow of action to focus lovingly on a particular tableau that is considered especially moving or auspicious—here, the death of monkey-king Bali in Ram's presence. This meter recurs periodically in the *Mānas,* and there have already been several instances of it in these three sub-books.

17 "Thorny acacia," *babūra;* a common variety of tree found throughout South Asia.

18 Both swallowwort (*arka,* also known as *madār*) and camel thorn (*javās*) are wild, bushy plants, generally regarded as noxious weeds, although both have medicinal uses in Ayurveda. Their seasonal cycle is the reverse of that of many plant species in India, which shed their leaves during the hot weather and gain new ones with the coming of the rains. Tulsi compares their bareness to the inability of wicked people to carry on their misdeeds under a virtuous regime.

19 According to commentators, just as travelers are unable to reach their destinations on flooded roads, so the bodily senses of a spiritually wise person are weakened and cannot go toward sensory objects.

20 "Plumes of reeds," *kāsa;* a tall grass native to the subcontinent, it blooms profusely on floodplains after the monsoon, producing waving, grayish-white plumes.

21 "Wagtail," *khañjana;* the white-browed wagtail, or large pied wagtail, is a bird indigenous to the subcontinent.

22 "Dependent kin," *abudha kuṭumbī;* although *abudha* is generally translated "stupid" or "dull," I agree with commentators who take the sense here to be of hanger-on relations who do not work to restore a family's fortunes; see *Mānaspīyūṣ* 5.2.163–164.

23 "Those in life's four stages," *āśramī cāri;* this refers to the four traditional phases of life: student, married householder,

contemplative retiree, and total renunciant. According to commentators, their "arduous effort" (*śrama*) refers to conventional religious practices such as sacrifice, mantra repetition, yoga, and so on.

24 "Ruddy goose," *cakrabāka;* this species of bird is believed to suffer separation from its mate at nightfall, and is thought to be jealous of other species that delight in the postmonsoon nights.

25 "Pied cuckoo," *cātaka;* this migratory bird, also called the Jacobin cuckoo, is said to arrive at the onset of the rainy season and to live only on raindrops; hence it suffers when the monsoon ends.

26 Alternatively, this half *caupāī* verse may be read as referring to three categories of people who can understand Ram's acts: "sages, enlightened ones, and those committed to loving the Raghu hero's feet."

27 These are said to be counsel that is gentle and conciliatory (*sāma*), speaks to one's profit (*dāma*), warns of punishment (*daṇḍa*), and causes doubt or disunity (*bheda*).

28 Literally, this quarter *caupāī* verse says that Hanuman "showed them fear, affection, and instruction."

29 "Amicably extended his hand," *abhaya bāṇha tehi dīnhī;* literally, "gave him his arm of not-fear"—because Ram had promised the dying Bali that he would look after his son.

30 This ends the apparent aside from Shiva signaled by the vocative ("Uma"), though he is also narrating the story to her.

31 Apparently others were summoned as well, as the next verse shows. They included Nil, brother of Nal, and Jambavan, the king of bears, who first appears in the narrative here.

32 Literally, "One serves the sun with one's back, and fire with one's chest." This apparent aphorism contrasts the respect and caution shown when warming oneself by means of these two elemental forces with the unconditional (*sarba bhāva*) service owed to a master.

33 "Kingly protocol," *rājanīti;* that is, Ram followed prudent worldly practice in dispatching messengers to look for Sita.

34 Presumably, this was to inquire whether the sage knew anything of Sita's whereabouts, although some commentators observe that they may also have been examining him to ascertain that he was not a demon in disguise.

35 Tulsi omits most details of the story of Svayamprabha, the demidivine woman who was instructed, long before, to live in

this enchanted underground realm until Ram took birth in the Treta Yuga (see the *Vālmīki Rāmāyaṇa* 4.49.30–52.13; Lefeber 1994: 163–168). Her account usually includes the detail that no one who enters the cavern can ever leave it. However, here she promises to magically transport the monkeys out with their eyes closed (as the next line notes).

36 "The forest of Badri," ***badarībana;*** a Himalayan pilgrimage place, sacred to Vishnu, now known as Badrinath.

37 *Darbha* grass, also known as *kuśa*, has been used in ritual since Vedic times. Spreading it is considered to purify the ground for a ritual undertaking—in this case, the monkeys' intended fast unto death.

38 Since vultures do not eat living beings, Sampati evidently perceives that the monkeys intend suicide.

39 "Funerary offering," ***tilāñjali;*** literally, "a handful of sesame seeds," which are poured into a body of water as an offering to departed souls.

40 "League," ***jojana;*** the vague, obsolete English unit works well for an ancient Indian one variously defined as four, eight, or sixteen miles. In any case, a hundred of them would represent a formidable distance.

41 The vocative signals that the foregrounded narrator here (appropriately, recounting an episode concerning a bird) is the immortal crow Bhushundi, speaking to Garuda.

42 In an oft-told puranic story, Bali (an ancient demonic king, not to be confused with Sugriv's brother Bali) offered a boon to Vaman, a Brahman dwarf who was actually Vishnu incarnate. When the latter requested only as much land as he could cover in three strides, the king was amused and readily agreed. The dwarf then grew to cosmic proportions and, in three steps, took back the entire universe that the demon had conquered. With his third footfall, he pushed the gods' enemy into the netherworld.

43 "Incarnation," ***avatāra;*** Jambavan's use of this word is understood by many to refer to Hanuman being an embodiment of Rudra, an energetic and sometimes destructive form of Shiva. Significantly, it is this invocation that causes the great monkey to grow to immense size, break his silence, and pledge to undertake the mission.

44 The final verses of this stanza are in *harigītikā chand* meter and

begin, according to Tulsi's usual practice, with a reiteration of the final *caupāī* verse.

*The Beautiful Quest*

1 As is traditional, the first verses of this sub-book are a Sanskrit invocation (*maṅgalācaraṇa*). In this case, the first two praise Ram and the third pays special tribute to Hanuman, whose heroic deeds dominate this sub-book.

2 Vedanta (literally, "the end/concluding portion of the Veda") is generally understood to refer to a nondualist philosophy based on the teachings of the Upanishads. Although some Vaishnavas reject the radical monism of Vedantic thought, Tulsidas generally shows sympathetic respect for it, even as he celebrates the devotee's loving relationship to a decidedly tangible and embodied Ram.

3 "Mind," *mānasa;* significantly, Tulsi also invokes the abbreviated title of his poem, permitting the reading "purge my *Mānas* of lust and other flaws."

4 This verse in praise of Hanuman occurs, in old and respected manuscripts, with variants in its first and last lines. The first is the substitution of *svarṇa* for *hema,* but since both mean "gold," the meaning ("with a body like a gleaming mountain of gold") is unaffected. The second variant, however, replaces the phrase *raghupati vara dūtaṃ* ("chosen emissary of the Raghu lord") with *raghupati priya bhaktaṃ* ("beloved devotee of the Raghu lord"). Although the latter reading is found in Gita Press editions, I have used the former (which appears, uncharacteristically without any comment on the variant, in the *Mānaspīyūṣ*), both because it seems to better suit the narrative content of *Sundarkāṇḍ* and because it was favored by several traditional *Mānas* scholars with whom I studied.

5 The Avadhi text begins with this *caupāī* verse, which returns to the scene at the conclusion of the previous sub-book: the bear Jambavan has just reminded Hanuman of his divine birth and powers and enjoined him to leap the sea to Lanka.

6 According to epic and puranic myth, both the ocean god and Mainak were seeking to discharge old debts by offering this service. The ocean's depths were excavated by the sixty thousand sons of Ram's ancestor King Sagar, and then filled with water when Bhagirath, Sagar's great-grandson, brought the celestial Ganga down to earth. In another tale, mountains originally possessed wings and

could move about at will, until Indra cut off their wings with his thunderbolt, rendering them immobile. However, Hanuman's father, the wind god Vayu, took pity on Mount Mainak and hid him in the ocean's depths, and hence this peak alone remained capable of movement.

7 In most Ramayana retellings, this subterranean she-demon is identified as Simhika (*siṃhikā*). Though she succeeds, by seizing Hanuman's shadow, in drawing him into her maw, he bursts out of her stomach, leaving her dead.

8 "Surely...be saved," *gati paihahī sahī;* since the last word may be taken as either an adjective or adverb ("true" or "truly"), this may also be read as "they will attain true salvation."

9 "Man-lion," *narahari;* one of the demon-slaying avatars of Vishnu. Since this phrase can also mean "Hari (Vishnu) in human form," it may also be read as an epithet of Ram.

10 Since her name ("[woman] of Lanka") derives from that of the city, it is usually assumed that she is its protective tutelary goddess (*bhū devī*), whose shrine is located at one of the city gates, where she guards against unwanted intruders. In a succeeding verse, Tulsi calls her simply "Lanka." Commentators attach great significance to her transformation after meeting Hanuman, asserting that she then abandons her post, signaling the approaching doom of Ravan and his kingdom.

11 Ravan and his brothers, desiring immortality, had performed severe austerities to win Brahma's grace. As a result, the demon was granted the boon of immunity from death at the hands of gods, demons, and demidivine beings; see *Rāmcaritmānas* 1.177 (volume 2, pp. 3–5, in *The Epic of Ram*).

12 This interjected aside reminds us that, among the epic's several narrators, the immortal crow Bhushundi is recounting the tale to Garuda, Vishnu's avian vehicle.

13 "Set apart," *bhinna banāvā;* this suggests the custom, common among wealthy Hindu families today, of situating a small shrine in the garden of a palatial home. However, one commentator has noted that this can also be interpreted to mean "differently designed"—that is, not resembling other structures in Lanka (*Mānaspīyūṣ* 6.1.65).

14 Although commentators attribute this assertion to Hanuman's devotional humility, they point out his shift, in this line, from the first-person singular to plural, indicating that he is speaking of

the general baseness of monkeys as a species. Invoking Hanuman himself in morning worship, they note, is highly auspicious. See *Mānaspīyūṣ* 6.1.80–81.

15 As noted in the preceding sub-books, in the Ramayana context the tree's Sanskrit name, *aśoka,* is ironic because it means "without sorrow."

16 Here Tulsi lists the four traditional ways of manipulating an adversary according to ancient treatises on politics: conciliation (*sāma*), gifts (*dāna*), instilling fear (*bhaya*), and sowing discord within an alliance (*bheda*).

17 This half line may also be read as a question: "Do you not know of the Raghu hero's arrows?"

18 Chandrahas (literally, "moon smile") is the name of Ravan's legendary sword.

19 "Your gleaming blade flows cool and keen," *sītala nisita bahasi baradhārā;* according to the *Mānaspīyūṣ* (6.103–104), some early manuscripts offer a variant on this half line, yielding the reading, "Blade, your lovely flow is [like] cool night" (*sītala nisi tava asi baradhārā*).

20 "Before many days," *gaẽ dina cārī;* literally, "when four days have passed," however, the expression is commonly used to denote an indeterminate but short period of time.

21 "For my disease is terminal," *jani karahi nidānā;* literally, "do not let [my disease] reach its ultimate conclusion." There is a variant text in some early manuscripts, however, and the *Mānaspīyūṣ* favors "give me fire and put an end to this body" (*dehi agini tana karahi nidānā*); see 6.1.119.

22 Sita's response is usually said to be owing to both the general inauspiciousness of monkeys and her suspicion that her visitor might actually be the wily Ravan in disguise.

23 "Loving speech," *bacana saprema;* as the *Mānaspīyūṣ* points out, *saprema* here ("with love") may refer to both Hanuman's speech and the manner in which Sita received it (6.1.129).

24 The Gita Press and *Mānaspīyūṣ* texts vary over the end words in each half of this *ardhālī*, with the latter favoring *harijana jāni prīti ati bāṛhī / sajala nayana pulakāvali ṭhāṛhī* ("Knowing him as the Lord's, her love swelled, / her eyes filled with tears as her body thrilled with joy"; 6.1.130). However, the difference hardly affects the meaning; either way, they describe the physical manifestations of Sita's intense love.

25 "Ram's love for you exceeds even yours," *tumha te premu rāma kẽ dūnā;* literally, "Ram's love for you is double your own."

26 "Branch-beasts," *sākhāmṛga;* the literal translation of this synonym for "monkey" is used here to suggest the pejorative thrust of Hanuman's evaluation of his species.

27 "Bared his teeth," *kaṭakaṭāi;* this onomatopoetic word invokes the clicking sound anthropoid primates make with their teeth when facing a potential enemy, and it is frequently used by Tulsi in the epic's battle scenes. Since English usage tends to associate the clicking or chattering of teeth with feeling cold, "baring" (or, elsewhere, "gnashing") seems a preferable translation.

28 Commentators observe that Hanuman (whom they consider an avatar of Shiva) was not, in fact, unconscious but only "showing respect for the Brahma weapon," as previous verses explained, and that Tulsi's use of the verb "to see" refers solely to the demon's (false) perception; see *Mānaspīyūṣ* 6.1.173.

29 "The whole cosmos," *aṇḍakosa;* literally, "pod of eggs." In ancient Indian cosmology, this term was used to connote the multiple worlds and star systems understood to constitute the universe.

30 The three brothers Khar, Dushan, and Trishira were foremost among Ravan's minions who were slain by Ram in *Aranyakāṇḍ* (3.18–20a); Bali was the monkey king killed by Ram at Sugriv's behest in *Kiṣkindhākāṇḍ* (4.8).

31 Hanuman is renowned for his eloquence, and here Tulsi (who generally expresses himself in grammatically self-contained half *caupāī* verses) gives him one of the longest sentences in the entire *Mānas*—a string of relative clauses that runs (in this version) for twelve lines, until the main clause arrives in this *dohā* verse.

32 "Monkey jabs," *kapi bacana;* literally, "monkey speech," but Hanuman's words are clearly pejorative. "Laughed evasively," *bihãsi baharāvā;* the second word (in modern Hindi the verb *bahlānā,* literally meaning "to make something flow away" and figuratively, "to divert one's mind") suggests Ravan's attempt to distract his courtiers by seeming to laugh off Hanuman's sarcasm, since in both of the encounters mentioned—with the prodigious human king Sahasbahu, and with the powerful monkey lord Bali—Ravan was ignominiously defeated.

33 Commentators note that Hanuman's use, in addressing Ravan, of apparently respectful vocatives normally reserved for Ram (*prabhu* and *svāmī*—here translated "Your Lordship" and "sir")

simply reflects the proper protocol for a royal messenger when in an enemy's court (*Mānaspīyūṣ* 6.1.187).

34 Tulsi previously advanced this metaphorical argument, expressive of his culture's high valuation of *śṛṅgāra,* or adornment, at *The Epic of Ram, Volume 1,* p. 29 and *Rāmcaritmānas* 1.10.2, to support his contention that poetry that does not contain the name of Ram lacks beauty.

35 Hanuman reasons that Sarasvati, goddess of speech and intelligence, has put the idea of burning his tail into Ravan's mind, which Hanuman will now turn to Ram's advantage.

36 "Forty-nine winds," ***maruta unacāsa;*** according to puranic myth, the Maruts are angry storm winds that were created when Indra cut the fetus of a primal matriarch, Diti, into forty-nine pieces, in order to prevent the birth of a powerful half brother to himself.

37 "Crest jewel," ***cūṛāmaṇi;*** an ornament worn on the crown of a diadem or tiara adorning the head of a married royal woman.

38 The story of Jayant's attack on Sita and punishment by Ram is found at the beginning of *Araṇyakāṇḍ* (see 3.1–2).

39 "Joyful shriek," ***kilikilā;*** in this context, commentators interpret the onomatopoeic word as representing the sound that monkeys make when happily excited.

40 Royal Madhuban Grove, ***madhubana;*** literally, "honey grove." This is said to have been a private preserve of the Kishkindha royal family, containing heavenly fruit trees and flowers.

41 "The task is more than done," ***bhā kāju bisesī;*** literally, the task has been completed "in a special way," because in burning Lanka, Hanuman did even more than he was charged to do.

42 According to the *Mānaspīyūṣ,* the speaker is Jambavan, the venerable bear (6.1.242). Alternatively, the line could be read "and saved the lives of all of us monkeys."

43 The eyes are considered to be among the body's "nine portals" and a principal route through which life-energy (***prāna;*** here translated "spirit") may move. Sita's accusation against her eyes continues in the verse that follows, wherein they are said to weep out of self-interest. Commentators explain that this is because they crave sight of Ram (see *Mānaspīyūṣ* 6.1.254–255).

44 ***Sanamukha hoi na sakata mana morā;*** literally, "facing you, my mind cannot be." Commentators offer several interpretations for this enigmatic line, all of which suggest Ram's inability to conceive of any way of repaying Hanuman for his service.

45 "Save me," *trāhi;* this Sanskrit imperative form of a verb meaning to save or protect is preserved in Hindi as a formulaic cry for divine assistance. Directed toward Ram as the supreme God of Vaishnavas (*bhagavant*), it is taken by many commentators to signal Hanuman's humility and his desire to be "saved" from the sin of pride in having been praised so fulsomely by Ram.

46 To most traditional commentators, Shiva's "recollection" and ensuing state of bliss confirm that Hanuman is an avatar of Rudra, one of Shiva's powerful aspects.

47 "Branch-dwelling beasts," *sākhāmṛga;* Hanuman again uses this synonym for monkeys (see 5.16 and and note 26 in this section) that seems dismissive and self-effacing.

48 "Fire of world's-end," *baṛavānala;* the fire destined to consume the universe at the end of a cosmic cycle. Until then, it remains confined in the head of a mare at the bottom of the sea. Hanuman's hyperbolic claim is interpreted by most commentators as implying that something dry and easily flammable (a wisp of cotton) could itself, through a divine miracle, "consume" the most awful of conflagrations.

49 "Dialogue," *saṃvāda;* according to the *Mānaspīyūṣ,* Shiva's promise of spiritual benefit from certain verses (to "place a text in the heart" conventionally means to memorize it) refers to lines 5.33.3–34.1.

50 In Tulsi's account, the ordinary gods—like some spectators at modern *Rāmlīlā* plays—turn up for certain "high points" in the story but otherwise luxuriate in their celestial realms (though, in other contexts, we are told that they have been enslaved by Ravan).

51 This line carries a special resonance through its mythological associations: the great monkeys are called "monkey-Indras" and the winged mountains "mountain-Indras," hinting at the ancient story in which Indra, foremost of Vedic heroes, cut off the wings that all mountains once possessed (see note 6 in this section). According to some commentators, the monkeys acquire the power of flight at this point.

52 The *Mānaspīyūṣ* text varies slightly from that of Gita Press in the second line of the quatrain; the latter omits the sun and moon, substituting a word meaning "assembly" and *gandharvas,* a category of demigods who are celestial musicians (*mana haraṣa sabha gandharba sura*). Both readings are found in old manuscripts,

and their meanings are essentially the same: various categories of supernaturals rejoice because their liberation from Ravan's tyranny is imminent. But to me, the *Mānaspīyūṣ* version reads better in translation, hence I have substituted it in the Devanagari text.

53 In Hindu myth, the earth or cosmos is commonly said to rest on the thousand hoods of Shesh, the divine king of cobras, who, in turn, is coiled atop an immense tortoise that anchors the universe. The *Mānaspīyūṣ* notes that the complex simile of inscription found in this beautiful *chand* is modeled on a similar passage in the Sanskrit play *Hanumānnāṭaka* 7.3–4 (see *Mānaspīyūṣ* 6.1.287).

54 "Arrogantly," *mamatā adhikāī.* Since *mamatā* (literally, "my-ness") can connote both selfishness and affection, some commentators gloss this line as "making a great display of affection, he strode off to court."

55 According to commentators, the reference is specifically to a prohibition against looking at the moon on the fourth evening of the bright half of the month of Bhadrapad (August/September). For explanatory stories and ritual lore, see *Mānaspīyūṣ* 6.1.308–309.

56 Literally, "You forever live, scoundrel, by my causing you to live." Tulsi's ingenious and untranslatable use of the verb *jīnā* (to live) together with its causative form conveys the sense of Ravan's material sustenance and emotional indulgence of his younger brother.

57 Such abrupt insertions of asides from one of the four narrators, signaled only by a vocative identifying his listener (note that neither "Shiva said" nor "Vibhishan cried" appears in the Hindi text), are frequent reminders of the multiple narrative frames of the *Mānas.*

58 "Doomed," *āyū hīna;* literally, "without life." The next verse offers another comment by Shiva, signaled only by the vocative "Bhavani."

59 The reference is to the liberation from a curse of Ahalya, wife of the sage Gautam, in the epic's first sub-book; see *The Epic of Ram, Volume 2,* pp. 73–75 and *Rāmcaritmānas* 1.210.6–1.211.

60 "Lord of Lanka," *laṅkesa;* commentators note that, by addressing Vibhishan in this way, Rama predicts and indeed effects his succession as king of the *rākṣasas;* see *Mānaspīyūṣ* 6.1.361.

61 "Three kinds of worldly pain," *tribidha bhava sūlā.* These are

generally understood to be physical pain, pain caused by divine forces, and pain caused by evil spirits and sorcery.

62 "Relinquishing," *taji;* since this verb can also mean "ignoring" or "overlooking," there is ambiguity as to the agent of this half line: the asylum seeker (who abandons these bad qualities), or the welcoming Lord (who disregards them).

63 Water is essential in nearly all Hindu rituals, and here it is intended for the lustration that accompanies the consecration of a king, together with marking his brow with a *tilaka,* or auspicious sign.

64 "The wind of his own breaths," *nija śvāsa samīra.* There is disagreement among commentators as to the referent of the reflexive pronoun "one's own" (*nija*). Although most take it (as I do) to refer to Vibhishan, who had enraged Ravan with his gentle, sagacious words (here likened to wind fanning flames), some think it refers to Ravan or to Ram. The latter is the apparent subject of the second line of the couplet, which more literally reads, "[he] rescued Vibhishan, [who was] burning, and gave him endless dominion." However, I have made this passive to avoid an awkward shift in subject.

65 "Most modest gift," *sakuci dīnhi;* literally, "gave hesitantly or embarrassedly." In one interpretation, since the glory of the demons is tainted by their cruelty and violence, the Lord bestows this worldly favor on Vibhishan, his devotee, unpretentiously and with a certain diffidence. For extended discussion, see *Mānaspīyūṣ* 6.1.386–388.

66 "Linked to your lineage," *kulagura;* although the text literally calls him "an elder/teacher of your clan," the reference seems to be to the excavation of the seabed by the sons of Ram's ancestor King Sagar in their search for their father's sacrificial stallion; hence the ocean owes an ancient debt to the Raghu line.

67 "Fortune," *daiva;* literally, "of the gods," it may also be rendered as "destiny" or "fate."

68 "Deface us," *hara nāsā kānā;* literally, "remove our nose and ears." Such mutilation was a common form of nonlethal punishment. The spies plead for mercy, swearing an oath (*ānā*) on Ram's name.

69 "A wretched worm in grain bound for grinding," *java kara kīṭa abhāgī;* literally, "an ill-fated barley worm or maggot." The word meaning "ill-fated" implies that this insect will perish when the grain is ground into flour.

70 Some commentators do not take Ravan's name in the second line

of this couplet to be a vocative, yielding the reading, "and at their head is Lord Ram / who can best not only you, Ravan, but Death himself / a billionfold on any field!"

71 This is a mark of disrespect, since the left hand is considered impure.

72 This seeming aphorism, so offensive to many modern readers, has been subject to much analysis by commentators (see, for example, *Mānaspīyūṣ* 6.1.432–438), some of whom point to the several meanings of the verb *tāṛnā* (to punish, to beat, to chide, to admonish)—thus one "beats" a drum but merely "rebukes" a (wayward) villager, low-caste peasant, or woman. Given the fact that the verse begins with "drum," then includes three categories of traditionally disenfranchised human beings, along with livestock, and also sarcastically invokes the prestigious word *adhikārī* (connoting someone who is "deserving of" or "entitled to" something) as well as the context in which it is spoken, I have chosen not to blunt, in straightforward translation, its advocacy of physical domination to elicit obedience. For further discussion of the controversy this verse has generated, see Lutgendorf 1991: 396–403.

73 "My stature will suffer," *na mori baṛāī.* The phrase literally means "my greatness will not [be/endure]," and most commentators take this to refer to the ocean's divinely ordained attributes (of immensity and fathomlessness), of which he has just spoken. Some interpret the verb form in the following half *caupāī* verse as imperative, yielding "so quickly do whatever will please you."

74 In a passage found in many manuscripts of the *Vālmīki Rāmāyaṇa* (though omitted from the main text of its critical edition), the ocean god identifies the "sinners" as "savage tribes, Ābhīras, etc.," and some interpret the geographical reference as invoking a desert area in present-day Rajasthan; see Goldman, Sutherland Goldman, and van Nooten 2009: 614–615 (note on 6.15.7).

75 "All those misdeeds," *sakala carita;* most commentators assume this refers to the crimes of the northern shore-dwelling sinners whom Ram has just slain, but some interpret it as including reports of the misdeeds of the demons of Lanka.

# GLOSSARY

*aśoka* an evergreen tree regarded as sacred and auspicious; the garden in which Ravan imprisons Sita contains a grove of these trees, whose name is ironically understood to mean "without sorrow" (*a-śoka*)

AVADH (*avadha;* unconquerable) the kingdom and city of Ayodhya

*bakul* a tropical evergreen tree known for its thick foliage and fragrant blossoms

*brahma* the transcendent Supreme Being of Hindu philosophy, not to be confused with the creator god, Brahma

*cakor* the chukar partridge that, according to legend, forever craves the sight of the moon and feeds on its beams (and occasionally on fire); a poetic trope for fervent lovers and devotees

*campak* a large tree of the magnolia family that bears fragrant yellow flowers

GARUDA (*garuṛa*) a gigantic mythical bird, variously associated with the eagle, crane, or vulture species, who serves as the mount of Lord Vishnu

GAURI (*gaurī;* fair, light-complexioned) Parvati

*haṃsa* mythical bird that lives in the Himalayas, feeds on pearls, and has the ability to separate milk from water; a literary trope for the enlightened soul, it is often depicted by Tulsidas flying above or floating on Lake Manas; sometimes identified with the bar-headed goose that breeds in Central Asia and winters in India, crossing the Himalayas in its annual migrations

*kadamb* a tropical evergreen tree known for its fragrant orange blossoms

MARICH (*mārīca*) the name of a prominent demon, said to be an uncle of Ravan and one of the sons of Taraka defeated by Ram in sub-book one; in *Araṇyakāṇḍ* he is forced by Ravan to assume the form of a golden deer to lure Ram away from Sita

MAYA (*māyā;* fabrication, semblance) the illusory power of the gods, often personified as a goddess

MEGHNAD (*meghanāda;* thunderclap) Ravan's eldest son, also known as Indrajit (vanquisher of Indra)

RAMCHANDRA (*rāmacandra;* Ram, the moon) epithet of Ram, highlighting his beauty

*śarad* early autumn, the name of one of the traditional six seasons of the Indian year; it follows the rains and precedes the onset of colder weather

SHARADA (*śāradā,* autumnal) epithet of Sarasvati, goddess of speech, art, and learning and the wife of the creator-god Brahma

SUTIKSHAN (*sutīkṣṇa*) a forest-dwelling sage and a disciple of the great seer Agastya

*tamāl* also known as the Indian bay tree, an evergreen whose aromatic leaves are used in traditional medicine and cooking

VAIDEHI (*vaidehī;* daughter of Videha) epithet of Sita

# BIBLIOGRAPHY


*Editions and Translations*

*Kalyāṇ Mānasāṅk.* 1938. Edited by Hanuman Prasad Poddar. Commentary by Chimanlal Gosvami and Nanddulare Vajpeyī. Gorakhpur: Gita Press.

*Mānaspīyūṣ.* 1950. Edited by Anjaninandansharan. 7 vols. Gorakhpur: Gita Press.

*Rāmcaritmānas.* 1962. Edited by Vishvanath Prasad Mishra. Ramnagar, Varanasi: All-India Kashiraj Trust.

*Tulsī granthāvalī, pratham khaṇḍ,* vol. 1: *Rāmcaritmānas.* 1973. Edited by Ramchandra Shukla et al. Varanasi: Nāgarīpracāriṇī Sabhā.

Atkins, A. G., trans. 1954. *The Ramayana of Tulsidas.* 2 vols. New Delhi: Birla Academy of Art and Culture.

Bahadur, Satya Prakash, trans. 1978. *Rāmcaritmānas.* Varanasi: Prācya Prakāśan.

Dev, Satya, trans. 2010. *Tulsi Ramayan in English Verse.* New Delhi: Vitasta Publishing.

Dhody, Chandan Lal, trans. 1987. *The Gospel of Love: An English Rendering of Tulasi's Shri Rama Charita Manasa.* New Delhi: Siddharth Publications.

Goswami, Chimanlal, trans. 1949. *Śrīrāmacaritamānasa.* Gorakhpur: Gita Press.

Growse, Frederick Salmon, trans. 1978. *The Rāmāyaṇa of Tulasīdāsa.* New Delhi: Motilal Banarsidass. Original edition, Kanpur: E. Samuel, 1891.

Hill, W. Douglas P., trans. 1952. *The Holy Lake of the Acts of Rāma.* London: Oxford University Press.

Lutgendorf, Philip, trans. 2016. *The Epic of Ram.* Vols. 1 and 2. Cambridge, Mass.: Harvard University Press.

———, trans. 2018. *The Epic of Ram.* Vols. 3 and 4. Cambridge, Mass.: Harvard University Press.

———, trans. 2020. *The Epic of Ram.* Vol. 5. Cambridge, Mass.: Harvard University Press.

——, trans. 2022. *The Epic of Ram.* Vol. 6. Cambridge, Mass.: Harvard University Press.

——, trans. 2023. *The Epic of Ram.* Vol. 7. Cambridge, Mass.: Harvard University Press.

Nagar, Shanti Lal, trans. 2014. *Shri Ramcharitmanas.* 3 vols. Delhi: Parimal Publications.

Prasad, R. C., trans. 1988. *Tulasidasa's Shriramacharitamanasa.* Delhi: Motilal Banarsidass.

*Other Sources*

Chhawchharia, Ajai Kumar, trans. 2010. *Adhyātma Rāmāyaṇa of Maharṣi Vedavyāsa.* 2 vols. Varanasi: Chaukhamba Surbharati Prakashan.

Gandhi, Mohandas K. 1968. *An Autobiography, or, The Story of My Experiments with Truth.* Translated by Mahadev Desai. Ahmedabad: Navjivan Publishing House. Original edition, 1927–1929.

Goldman, Robert P., and Sally J. Sutherland Goldman, trans. 1996. *The Rāmāyaṇa of Vālmīki: An Epic of Ancient India, Volume V: Sundarakāṇḍa.* Princeton: Princeton University Press.

Goldman, Robert P., Sally J. Sutherland Goldman, and Barend A. van Nooten, trans. 2009. *The Rāmāyaṇa of Vālmīki: An Epic of Ancient India, Volume VI: Yuddhakāṇḍa.* Princeton: Princeton University Press.

Lefeber, Rosalind, trans. 1994. *The Rāmāyaṇa of Vālmīki: An Epic of Ancient India, Volume IV: Kiṣkindhākāṇḍa.* Edited by Robert P. Goldman. Princeton: Princeton University Press.

Lutgendorf, Philip. 1991. *The Life of a Text: Performing the* Rāmcaritmānas *of Tulsidas.* Berkeley: University of California Press.

——, trans. 1994. "Sundarkand." *Journal of Vaisnava Studies* 2:4, 91–127.

——, trans. 1995. "*Ramcaritmanas:* From Book Five, the Beautiful Book." In *The Norton Anthology of World Masterpieces,* expanded edition, ed. Maynard Mack. New York: W. W. Norton, 1: 2316–2332.

——, 2000. "Dining Out at Lake Pampa: The Shabari Episode in Multiple Ramayanas." In *Questioning Ramayanas,* ed. Paula Richman, 119-136. New York: Oxford University Press.

——, trans. 2001. "From the Ramcaritmanas of Tulsidas, Book Five: Sundar Kand." *Indian Literature* 45, 3 (203): 143–181.

——, 2007. *Hanuman's Tale: The Messages of a Divine Monkey.* New York: Oxford University Press.

Macfie, John Mandeville. 1930. *The Ramayan of Tulsidas, or, The Bible of Northern India.* Edinburgh: T. & T. Clark.

McGregor, Stuart. 2003. "The Progress of Hindi, Part 1." In *Literary Cultures in History: Reconstructions from South Asia,* ed. Sheldon Pollock, 912–957. Berkeley: University of California Press.

Monier-Williams, Monier. 1960. *A Sanskrit-English Dictionary.* Reprint of new edition, enlarged and improved, in collaboration with E. Leumann, C. Cappeller, et al. Oxford: Clarendon Press. First published 1899.

Orsini, Francesca. 1998. "Tulsī Dās as a Classic." In *Classics of Modern South Asian Literature,* ed. Rupert Snell and I. M. P. Raeside, 119–141. Wiesbaden: Harrassowitz.

Pollock, Sheldon I., trans. 1986. *The Rāmāyaṇa of Vālmīki: An Epic of Ancient India, Volume II: Ayodhyākāṇḍa.* Edited by Robert P. Goldman. Princeton: Princeton University Press.

——, trans. 1991. *The Rāmāyaṇa of Vālmīki: An Epic of Ancient India, Volume III: Araṇyakāṇḍa.* Edited by Robert P. Goldman. Princeton: Princeton University Press.

Stasik, Danuta. 2009. "Perso-Arabic Lexis in the *Rāmcaritmānas* of Tulsīdās." *Cracow Indological Studies* 11: 67–86.